# AFRO-AMERICAN ART AND CRAFT

"...after the dust of centuries has passed over our cities, we will be remembered not for victories or defeats in battle or in politics but for our contribution to the human spirit."

John Kennedy

Bronze plaque, part of a series by Ed Wilson for the John F. Kennedy Memorial Park, Binghamton, New York, 1967/68. It includes excerpts from a speech of the President.

# AFRO-AMERICAN ART AND CRAFT

## JUDITH WRAGG CHASE

**VNR** **VAN NOSTRAND REINHOLD COMPANY**
NEW YORK    CINCINNATI    TORONTO    LONDON    MELBOURNE

Acknowledgment is made to the following publishers and individuals for permission to quote copyrighted material: Longman Group Ltd., London, England; Random House, Inc. — Alfred Knopf, Inc.; The World Publishing Co.; Harper & Row Publishers, Inc.; Dr. Dorothy Porter; Dr. Lorenzo D. Turner; Col. William M. Spencer.

Van Nostrand Reinhold Company Regional Offices:
New York  Cincinnati  Chicago  Millbrae  Dallas
Van Nostrand Reinhold Company International Offices:
London  Toronto  Melbourne
Copyright © 1971 by Judith Wragg Chase
Library of Congress Catalog Card Number 76-163485

Printed by Halliday Lithograph Corporation
Bound by Publishers Book Bindery, Inc.
Published by Van Nostrand Reinhold Company
450 West 33rd Street, New York, N.Y. 10001
Published simultaneously in Canada by
Van Nostrand Reinhold Ltd.
16  15  14  13  12  11  10  9  8  7  6  5  4  3  2  1

# PREFACE

Few artists or authors are completely satisfied with their work when it is finished. However, I learned long ago, as an art student, that one cannot spend a lifetime trying to perfect one work of art in order to achieve a masterpiece. There comes a time when one must say, "I have done the best I could on this particular piece and will try to do better next time." The same holds true for this present work.

What little has previously been written on the cultural history of Afro-Americans has been fragmentary. There have been books on African history, and some on African art; still others on black people in American history, a few on nineteenth- and twentieth-century Afro-American artists. But none of these presents the subject as a whole.

This book is intended to bind the various component parts together and to show their relationships to each other, so that the reader can visualize the Afro-American's cultural heritage as a continuous stream, from pre-historic Africa to the present day. With so broad a scope, it has been impossible to treat any one aspect in great depth. However, the chapters on slave-craftsmen in America contain much new material not published before.

Hopefully, this book will open up new avenues of scholarship that will inspire others and lead them to new discoveries. If I can fire the intellecual curiosity of young people to do more research in this much neglected field, my efforts will have been justified.

It is impossible to cite all those persons and organizations who have assisted me. I owe a great debt to patient librarians from Maine to South Carolina who helped me in my research, especially those at the Bowdoin College Library in Brunswick, Maine, and the Charleston County Library and the Charleston Library Society in Charleston, South Carolina; as well as to The Old Slave Mart Museum for making its valuable archives available to me.

My thanks go especially to Mr. Milo B. Howard, of the Alabama Department of Archives and History; to Mrs. W. G. Wallace, of Florence, South Carolina; to Miss Lois Moran of the American Crafts Council; and to all the other officials and individuals who supplied me with photographs. My own photographs of The Old Slave Mart Museum collection I owe to the generosity of the Board or Trustees of The Miriam B. Wilson Foundation, which operates the Museum. They allowed me free access to the collection, and to the art of Walter Johnson, an Afro-American photo-finisher of great skill.

I am also under obligation to those scholars who read the first draft of my manuscript and offered helpful suggestions: the late Dr. James A. Porter, Head of the Art Department, Howard University; Dr. Benjamin Quarles, History Department, Morgan State College; and Dr. Boniface Obichere, a Biafran teaching African History at the University of California, Los Angeles. It is impossible for me to express my appreciation adequately for the invaluable assistance given me by Dr. Robert Farris Thompson, Assistant Professor of Art History, Yale University, an expert on Yoruba art and culture, who shares my own particular interest in the diffusion and syncretism of African culture in the New World. Not only did he read and copiously annotate my manuscript, but kept up a lively correspondence with me for many months. From him I received answers to many puzzling questions, sound constructive criticism, as well as much-needed encouragement.

To Sara S. Landis I owe a debt of gratitude for all the help she has given me in so many ways, though I realize that the reality of this book will be thanks enough, since it was her idea from its inception.

Most of all I am indebted to the late Miriam B. Wilson, founder of The Old Slave Mart Museum, whose interest in the art and craft of Afro-Americans prevented many artifacts and much historical information from being lost to posterity; and to Mrs. Louise A. Graves, Director of the Museum, whose vision saved this valuable collection from extinction and at whose urging I began my career in Negro history and art.

Lastly, I have been sustained constantly throughout this undertaking not only by my husband's unfailing patience and assistance, but above all by his faith and encouragement, which have helped me to sustain innumerable delays and difficulties.

Judith Wragg Chase

# CONTENTS

# INTRODUCTION

In tracing the antecedents of American art, conventional art histories dwell long on Egypt, then swing northward and eastward through Mesopotamia, Crete, Greece, and thence to Rome, England, and America. This is certainly one way by which art influences have reached this country, but it ignores the impressive contributions made by Africa to our American culture. This neglect is particularly tragic in the case of American Negro youth, for no one can fully understand his present, nor direct his future, without knowing something about his past, and the Afro-American has been unaware of his ancestral heritage for much too long.

Much of the blame for this lies in the appalling ignorance concerning Africa that has been almost universal until recently. The African interior remained "the dark continent" until the nineteenth century, because it was unexplored and unknown to Europeans. The Christian missions and colonialism that followed exploration encouraged a patronizing attitude toward African culture and did little to dissipate popular misconceptions about the continent. It was not until very recent years that the long history and cultural prominence of Black Africa began to be realized. Early travelers' accounts had given hints of the fabulous luxury of African courts in kingdoms such as that of ancient Ghana, but few people troubled to read them. It was reported that Kanissai, the King, ordered that his 10,000 horses should sleep only on precious rugs and be fettered with pure silk. He attached three persons to the chariot of each horse and provided them with bronze vessels in which to catch the sacred urine, a refinement certainly not found in European courts of that or any other era! Learning and culture were kept alive in Africa while Europe was enshrouded in its Dark Ages. Although the Atlantic slave trade and, later, colonialism were to bring a cultural eclipse to Africa in turn, this cannot erase the fact that there existed, at many different times and places on that continent, numerous highly developed cultures that compared favorably with the European ones of their day.

Until the twentieth century, most people accepted the belief that the American Negro had no past worth mentioning; that in any case his ancestors came from such widely scattered parts of Africa that none of his meager cultural inheritance could have survived. The anthropologist Melville J. Herskovits, who called this misconception "the myth of the Negro past," did much to dispel it in his book of the same name; so did such Negro scholars as Dr. W. E. B. Dubois, Dr. Carter G. Woodson, and Dr. John Hope Franklin. The rise of new African nations and the presence in this country of African diplomats and scholars have done even more to create a lively interest in African history and culture. These and other factors have brought about an encouraging change in attitudes and an appreciation for African art forms. In spite of this, however, knowledge of Africa remains fragmentary, and there seems to be little understanding of the true relationship of Africa to American art and culture.

In searching for African art influences in America, most people seem to expect them to be virtually unchanged. Since this does not often occur, the conclusion is that there is no influence. But just because no fire-spitter mask has been found in a former slave cabin, no Bambara antelope discovered amidst the carved decorations of a southern planter's mantelpiece, one cannot conclude that Africa has not left its mark on America.

Most components in a given culture—as they are diffused across neighboring areas or fragmented and carried to new localities—experience changes and adaptations due both to contact with other cultures as well as to environmental factors. This commonly occurred in Africa, where constant migrations of peoples from other continents, geographical changes, and technical developments created such fluid cultural patterns that the ultimate origin of their components cannot be traced with any certainty. These changes also took place when various cultural elements were transplanted to America from Europe and Africa. The picture is further confused by the fact that identical cultural patterns might have reached America from *both* Africa and Europe, because of a common Mediterranean origin. In any case, African forms and patterns were overlaid with those of the Dutch, English, German, or French slave-owners. In fact, imposition of European designs on the slave craftsman often left no room for "Africanisms" except in skill and techniques.

In discussing the technical ability and cultural traditions brought to this country by Negro slaves, however, we must take into consideration the area from which they came. This was a relatively narrow strip of Atlantic coastline extending from the Senegal River on the north to the southern (Namib) desert, called in slaving days "the Guinea Coast." Most of the slaves came from "Upper Guinea," which stretched around the hump of Africa from Senegambia on the north to Old Calabar on the Cross River. The 1,500 miles from Calabar to the southern desert was known as "Lower Guinea," and most of the slaves from this area were destined for the South American colonies of the Portuguese, who controlled slaving in the Kingdom of Kongo and in Angola. Many, however, also found their way to America, where "Ngolas," or "Gullahs," were among the most popular of the several sorts of Africans brought here in the eighteenth century.

The African interior featured little in the slave trade, for the greatest distance inland from which slaves were brought has been estimated to have been only a few hundred miles. There were exceptions, to be sure. One instance, cited by Herskovits, tells of a woman purchased at Cabinda, in Lower Guinea, who said she had come from another country "where the sun rises in the water and not, as in the Kongo, where it sets in the sea." This confirmed earlier reports by the Dutch geographer, Olfert Dapper, that slaves from Mozambique on the east coast were sometimes sold in the Kongo Kingdom, on the Atlantic coast. However, though this may prove that it was quite possible for a slave to have been handed across the continent from one trader to another—and no doubt they were occasionally—it was certainly not the general rule. A ready supply of slaves was too conveniently at hand quite close to the coast.

Nor did many Negroes reach America via the east-coast ports. This "Coast of Azania," or "Land of the Zanj," as it was variously called, enjoyed a thriving and peaceful trade for centuries. Our earliest firsthand report of this comes to us from a Greek mariner's guide, *The Periplus of the Erythraean Sea,* written about 60 A.D. From this and other evidence we know that such great east-coast trading centers as Sofala and Quelemane, or Pemba and Kilwa Islands, as well as Mombasa and Malindi, traded mainly with eastern markets from the Red Sea to China and Ceylon. The records show, too, that slaves were never a major item of export along this coast until the brief but bloody Arab slave trade from Zanzibar in the nineteenth century. Then, because of the international treaty banning the slave trade, many slavers from Europe or America sailed around the Cape of Good Hope to avoid the men-of-war patrolling the Guinea Coast. But this was so late in the history of the Atlantic slave trade that the number of east-coast Negroes involved was comparatively small. Thus, although few African peoples were spared some tribute of slaves, it is to the west coast that we must look for the major cultural contributions to America.

This geographical distinction is extremely important when we come to consider the artistic achievements of Afro-Americans, for art never reached the same degree of importance in every part of the African continent. Some tribal groups, such as the Masai in the east and the Zulu in the south, took more pride in their skill as warriors than they did in artistic pursuits. Others, such as the Mangbetu, between the headwaters of the Welle and Congo rivers, excelled in decorative or applied arts. Still others were best known for their pottery, for brass-casting, for leatherwork, or for weaving. Even in the earliest days contemporary sources show that certain communities had developed reputations as specialists in some particular handcraft. This was one of the factors in encouraging trade and communication between them. On the other hand, nomadic tribesmen throughout Africa were naturally reluctant to encumber themselves, so their art was apt to be restricted to the decoration of their persons or the most necessary of implements.

But the region from which most of the American Negro slaves were brought was one in which the artist-craftsman was highly regarded and one that produced some of the world's finest art, including the figure sculpture which has made African art justly famous. There, complex trading economies and theocratic states encouraged art to serve god, king, and man.

Transplanted to America, the African had less opportunity and motivation for artistic expression. Deprived of god and king, his art could no longer serve the world of the spirit or the court, and he had to content himself with serving man. This he did with consummate skill, and with as much creativity as was possible within the restrictive bonds of slavery. In this he was aided by the fact that even in Africa his works of art had been rigidly bound by traditional patterns and rules, and he was accustomed to finding individual ways of expressing himself within these bounds. Although he was stripped of his physical possessions, stripped of his cultural context, the African slave could not be stripped of his talent. He carried with him his expert skills and artistic sensitivity. Above all, he carried with him his capacity to adapt to changing circumstances, a quality that was to result in the development of new motives for artistic expression. These were to enrich both his own life and the lives of the Caucasian Americans with whom he was to make his future home.

Since the function of such art objects as masks and figure sculpture was to serve the religious and social needs of African societies, there was no longer any occasion for making them in the West-oriented society of the New World. Therefore, all during the slaveholding period the most common avenue of creativity open to the black people of America, whether slave or free, was in the handcrafting of necessary articles. This denied them an important emotional and spiritual mode of expression, but it was not altogether alien to their experience, since for centuries the African had excelled in producing beautiful functional articles for his own use or for trade.

The preindustrial culture to which the African was first introduced in America was one that held the expert craftsman in great respect, just as in African society. Because of the difficulty of importing goods from Europe, Americans depended largely on locally made utilitarian objects. In setting up a civilized society in the wilderness it was difficult to know what was needed most urgently. Furniture, tools, clothing? Or the buildings and ships, carts and carriages to house and carry them? Everything was needed, and quickly, and the well-trained, highly skilled African craftsmen worked side-by-side with his European counterparts in satisfying that demand.

Although this new culture was alien to the Negro slave, the work was familiar, since the materials available to him for artistic expression were often identical to those he was accustomed to using in Africa—wood, metal, natural fibers, animal products, clay, etc.—and many of the old-country techniques could be applied without change. But the African artist-craftsman also assimilated European techniques and ideas and melded them with those of his forefathers. Thus, the process of creative synthesis continued in this country as it had across the ocean, where the African had always borrowed much—from conqueror, from conquered, from new neighbors or traders, from ancestors—but had also invented much; through this invention and adaptation he had developed new cultures of his own.

Although the Afro-American slave produced many beautiful objects for everyday use, not all black people during slave days were confined to utilitarian handcrafts. As early as the eighteenth century there are records of American Negroes, both slave and free, who worked in the fields of painting, woodcarving, gold- or silversmithing, engraving or the allied art of wood-block printing. Although these vocations were also regarded as functional at that period, they offered more scope for the creative talents of the artist-craftsman than did the making of articles for use for the plantation. As the nineteenth century wore on, more and more Negroes distinguished themselves as painters and sculptors, though few achieved the recognition and acceptance to which they were entitled. Most of them encountered racial bias, and some were so embittered by it that they became expatriates. Yet, in spite of the difficulties encountered by all artists everywhere, and the additional handicap of racial prejudice, they succeeded to a remarkable degree.

The works of these artists followed the mainstream of art—at first somewhat stiff and formal and later often oversentimentalized. This, however, merely reflected the prevailing trend of the times, which turned from eighteenth-century formality to nineteenth-century Romanticism in reaction to the ugliness produced by the Industrial Revolution. The trend toward realism that developed near the end of the nineteenth century began to bring out the individuality of the Afro-American artist as he turned to subjects close at hand. The racial pride ignited by the "New Negro" movement of the 1920s did even more to produce an exciting collection of Afro-American art. Through it, the black artist, as well as Negro patrons, discovered greater pride of race and accomplishment. Through it, also, the black artist slowly and painfully began to achieve the recognition he deserved.

As American art in general became more individualistic and experimental, the Afro-American artist, too, began to discover more scope for his creative talents. Today we find him producing work in every imaginable field of art, out of every kind of material from junk to electronic equipment, and in many different styles and techniques. One of the most interesting of recent developments is that the Negro artist has begun to come full circle, back to functionalism once more. Originally a craftsman-artist, both in Africa and the early days of America, he was turned away from craftsmanship as a vocation through the snobbery of nineteenth-century art circles, which held the erroneous idea that handcrafts were necessarily crude, simple, and somehow less worth the efforts of a serious artist than were other fields. Fortunately, this view is fast disappearing. More and more American artists of all races are producing beautiful, sophisticated, contemporary handcrafts in a variety of media. The black artist is following this trend and making a rich contribution to the field of functional art.

Just as every American is a blend of many different cultures, so too is the modern black artist. However, he alone among them can claim an African inheritance. Unfortunately, American education has stressed his European heritage at the expense of his African one, and, in spite of improved understanding of the true role of black people in American history, the artistic work of the Afro-American remains greatly ignored and unappreciated today, except in the fields of music and the performing arts.

For a full appreciation of today's black artist and the valuable contributions made by his race to our American culture, we must understand his background. We must learn not only about the free and sophisticated artists of the nineteenth and twentieth centuries but also about the slave artisans who made the most of whatever opportunities for self-expression came their way. We must know something of the impact of Western cultural traditions—and the exigencies of a pioneer country—on his ancestors during the three hundred years since they first arrived in this country. We must also go back to the American Negro's ancestral beginnings in Africa. For out of this heritage the Afro-American artist is forging a dynamic art life of his own—a blend of cultures from three continents: Africa, Europe, and America.

This map of pre-colonial Africa clearly shows how cultural ideas from other continents were funneled via caravan routes towards the great Black kingdoms on the west coast. Some were brought to east-coast ports from China, India, and Indonesia, and then across the northern or southern Savannas; others crossed the Mediterranean from north or east before following the trade routes south across the Sahara.

Dotted lines represent trade routes. The numbers indicate the four principal caravan routes across the Sahara, as follows: (1) Taodeni Trail, (2) Gadames Trail, (3) Bilma Trail, (4) Selima Trail.

17

# 1  AFRICAN BACKGROUND

Bronze tusk holder, Benin, 17th century. Magnificent heads like this ornament the ancestral shrines of the Oba of Benin today, as they did when this was made. Beautifully carved elephant tusks rose from the top of the head. (Courtesy, The Museum of Primitive Art)

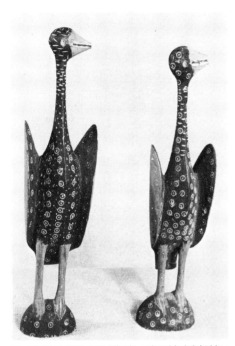

Carved wood birds from Liberia, painted in bright blue and red. The symbolic circle and dot design incised on the surface was used frequently in Africa. (Collection Old Slave Mart Museum. Photo, author)

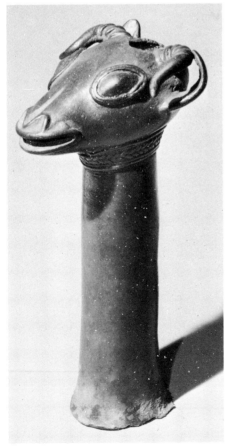

Bronze finial in the shape of ram's head. From Benin, Nigeria, about the middle of the 18th century. (Courtesy, The Museum of Primitive Art)

Because of the world's neglect, African history has been shrouded in a fog of ignorance that scholarship is only just beginning to dissipate. Archaeology is still in its infancy on the African continent, with the exception of Egypt, and archaeological research is needed for verification of oral histories. Written source material is still scarce, although more and more of it, long buried in obscure libraries, is now coming to light.

Still, here and there we do find a rift in the fog that allows us a tantalizing glimpse of Africa's ancient glories—of luxurious courts, profitable and far-reaching trade, highly organized societies; of conquest and expansion as well as worldwide respect.

All too often these fragmentary glimpses raise more questions than they answer. Consider, for example, the triangular niches discovered in ruined brickwork on the plains of Somalia. What link may there be between them and similar ones found at Kumbi Saleh, probable site of the capital of ancient Ghana, in faraway Mauritania? Is there a connection between the Divine Kingship of Egypt, of Zimbabwe in Rhodesia, and of numerous West African kingdoms? And what of the geometrical patterns and monoliths found both in stone ruins and graves near Amboim on the Angola coast and at Zimbabwe on the other side of the continent? Such symbols as the ram and the python, the circle and dot, appear in widely scattered localities throughout Africa. Where did they originate? Who taught whom? Or did these ideas spring up simultaneously in several places that had no contact with each other?

We may never know the answers to all such frustrating questions, but we can at least make some conjectures, and, as the tools of scholarship increase, so will our firm knowledge. At present we must try to fit together scattered bits and pieces in order to get some inkling of the Afro-American's ancestral story. Several important pieces of this jigsaw puzzle slipped into place recently when discoveries in the Sahara shed new light on ancient African peoples and cultures. On the Tassili Plateau of the Atlas Mountains, a French team under Henri Lhote discovered and painstakingly copied innumerable prehistoric paintings and engravings in the caves and canyons of that region. Scholars are now comparing them with prehistoric rock works in such widely scattered localities as Egypt and Libya; Nigeria and Cameroun; Ethiopia, Tanzania, and Angola; as well as Rhodesia and South Africa. This study has yielded new understanding of the peoples who inhabited the Sahara in ancient times and has helped to clarify the relationship between these Saharan peoples and those of other localities. The importance of the Sahara as the cradle of civilization on the African continent is now coming into focus.

The paintings copied by Lhote's team on the Tassili Massif are a veritable catalog of styles and periods. Layer was painted upon layer by successive peoples. Lhote and his co-workers identified at least sixteen different strata, and radiocarbon dating shows that these are among the earliest examples of African art, covering time periods that range from 10,000 B.C. to about 3000 B.C. In between, both wild and domestic animals jostle and overlap each other and the human inhabitants in a riot of color and animation that reaches the same level of artistic quality as the superb cave paintings of Altamira in Spain and Lascaux in France. The Tassili rock art also gives support to earlier scientific findings. By the 1930s, geologists, paleontologists, and archaeologists had clearly established the fact that after an early dry period the Sahara was, for some three thousand years, a fertile land. Its temperate climate supported an abundance of life. There were forests of oak, cypress, and other trees; its many rivers supplied a variety of fish, and its grassy plains abounded with wild game. Developing man, ever in search of subsistence, found his way into this rich country, where there began a fruitful mingling and multiplication of peoples and ideas, which, in turn, led to improvements in tools and techniques. The Saharan prehistoric paintings bear out these scientific findings. The ecological story is plain to see, for much of the animal life depicted by the rock paintings either is now extinct or has moved out of the region into moist areas farther south. In the earliest work, the long-horned buffalo, now extinct, appears amid tropical vegetation. Water-loving hippopotami, elephants, giraffes, ostriches, and okapi are there too. We can also follow early man as he moves out of the Stone Age into later stages of development. Human figures in the form of hunters appear, armed at first with bows and arrows and later with javelins and short stabbing swords. Domestic animals such as sheep illustrate the beginnings of animal husbandry around 3500 B.C. And the most recent periods show the horse, which was introduced into the Sahara about 1500 B.C., and the camel, brought in by the Romans between the third and sixth centuries B.C.

The exact identity of these people who inhabited the green Sahara is not clear, but, in any case, the rock paintings give convincing evidence that Negroes had occupied the Sahara at least as far north as the Tassili Plateau in very ancient times and that Negro peoples were producing lasting works of art by approximately 4000 B.C. Among Lhote's discoveries was a painting depicting masks that are much like those still carved by the Senufo people of the Ivory Coast. This suggests that these people originally lived much farther north. Other paintings in the Fezzan indicate a connection between the inhabitants there and the present-day Fulani, or Peul, who live in western Africa, along the fringes of the Sudan.

During the fertile period there must have been easy contact between the peoples of the Sahara and those of other regions; this led to a mingling of men and ideas. But, sometime before the fourth millennium B.C., the Sahara gradually began to lose its rainfall; the ensuing desiccation was to result finally in the desert barrier that we know today.

This formidable barrier, however, was never complete. Contact across the Sahara continued as raiding and trading routes were maintained, despite the rigors of desert travel. But it was a barrier, nevertheless, that effectively separated the peoples of North Africa from those who had moved south to escape the aridity. And, as the peoples developed separately, they developed differently.

Detail of prehistoric painting, Tassili Massif, North Africa. Some of these paintings are thought by scholars to date from 10,000 B.C. They show a variety of styles and subjects, and indicate a relationship between the peoples of the Sahara and the West African ancestors of American Negroes. (Courtesy, Professor Walter Deshler, University of Maryland)

As men deserted the dying Sahara in search of water, they settled first near the Mediterranean or along the Nile and Niger rivers. Later they spread out across the grassy savanna below the desert and split like two streams to skirt the tropical forests of Central Africa where agriculture was difficult. Settlements were established along the coasts of the Atlantic and Indian Oceans and down the Great Rift Valley in East Africa, as well as in both the northern and southern savannas. Later, when forest crops were introduced from Asia around the first century A.D., the Bantu expanded in a great arc through Central and Southern Africa from their settlements on the west coast. But of all these people, those who settled along the Nile appear to have developed the fastest.

The culture that evolved in ancient Egypt was, of course, one of the greatest and the best known of these early civilizations—so well known, in fact, that it need not be considered at length here. However, Egypt's outstanding advancement is usually ascribed to its Caucasian population, an assumption that is now being challenged. Probably founded by the same basic stock that peopled the green Sahara, and fed by additional migratory waves from Asia and the Near East, it is reasonable to assume that it contained a large element of negroid peoples. Also, it kept up a continuous interrelationship with its neighbors to the south, in so-called Black Africa, a contact that took place by means of either the Nile River or the caravan trails across the desert.

Directly south of Egypt, below the first cataract of the Nile, lay the rich lands of Nubia, known to the Egyptians as the Kingdom of Kush and to the early Greeks as *Ethiopia,* or the "land of the burnt faces." Still farther to the southwest lay the fabled countries of Axum and Punt, the Ethiopia and Somali Republic of today. All these cultures helped to supply Egypt with a rich stream of slave-labor, as well as quantities of gold, ivory, ebony, gums and perfumes, plus ostrich feathers, rare woods, precious stones, and the skins of wild animals.

Nubia, however, was not merely a source of profitable trade for Egypt; it was of far greater importance. This Kingdom of Kush, with its capital first at Napata, at the Nile's fourth cataract, and later at Meroë, just north of modern Khartoum, briefly attained the status of a world power in the eighth century B.C., and for many centures afterward it remained a thriving state that commanded the respect of the ancient world.

During the several centuries of almost continuous political domination by Egypt (from about 2950 to 1200 B.C.), Kush absorbed much of Egyptian culture, and Egypt was influenced in turn by its close contact with these black people. Nubians helped to construct Egypt's temples and tombs; they served in the Egyptian army and sent tribute to its Pharaohs. Egyptian hieroglyphs depict many dark-skinned men and women.

By 750 B.C., the Nubians had not only gained their independence but, under the leadership of their illustrious kings, Kashta and Piankhy, had conquered all of Lower Egypt. For one hundred years (ca. 750–655 B.C.), black Kushite pharaohs wore the double crown of Upper and Lower Egypt. They ruled from the Mediterranean to the borders of modern Ethiopia and possibly beyond—until the Assyrian invasion in the seventh century B.C. drove the Kushites back to the Upper Nile.

This Twenty-fifth Egyptian Dynasty of Kushitic pharaohs brought a flowering of the arts to Egypt and left behind a number of fine monuments. These include the great pylon in the State Temple to Amun at Karnak, and a papyrus column, some 80 feet high, built by King Taharqa. At Mediniet Habu, there still stands the mortuary chapel of Amenardis, high priestess of Amun and a princess of

Egyptian wall painting from the Tomb of Huy, Viceroy of Nubia, about 1355 B.C. Represents a delegation of Nubians presenting tribute to Pharaoh. (Courtesy, The Metropolitan Museum of Art)

Kush. It is composed of a columned court and a barrel-vaulted offering room with auxiliary chapels. These are only samplings of the contributions made by the Kushites to Egyptian art. But the greatest artistic achievement of the Nubians was the creation of a new and realistic trend in the art of portraiture in Egypt. Their astonishingly natural and individualistic figures have survived in large numbers and include a statue of King Taharqa that very clearly shows his negroid features.

Not long after the end of the Twenty-fifth Dynasty, probably around 530 B.C., the seat of Kushite power was transferred from the ancient capital of Napata to Meroë, farther south. What caused this shift is still unclear. No doubt the continuing desiccation of the Sahara was making itself felt. But it is also likely that there was another and more important reason—the Iron Age had arrived! For the Assyrians had defeated the Kushites with a new type of weapon—weapons made of tempered iron instead of bronze and stone.

The Egyptians and Nubians had known iron for many centuries but had prized it as a mere curiosity. They had made little attempt to master the intricacies of obtaining and working it. But after the Assyrian invasion, iron could no longer be ignored. It may have been this fact alone that transferred the seat of power from Napata to Meroë, which has large deposits of iron ore.

In any case, within a few hundred years of the coming of iron weapons the ironworkers of Meroë had turned their city into one of the greatest iron-founding centers of the ancient world and iron technology had spread like wildfire across Africa. With this development came a "Meroitic Renaissance" that gave birth to a civilization quite different from that of Egypt. Archaeology at Meroë is still in its infancy, but already we are beginning to appreciate the fact that Meroitic art is sufficiently distinctive to merit consideration and further study. It will be even better understood and appreciated when the key to its still undeciphered language is found.

Although Meroë's art was obviously influenced by Egyptian and Mediterranean cultures, the Kushites transformed the styles of those areas into an art that is distinctive and unmistakably Meroitic and added new elements of their own. All this can be seen in the well-rounded female figures, in highly individual pottery styles, and in the use of specific motifs and subjects. Prominent among the latter, for instance, are elephants and lions. These are seldom seen in Egyptian art. The lion, symbol of the Meroitic god Apedemek, occurs with particular frequency.

Pottery is one of the best known of Meroë's artistic products and is justly famed, not only for the quantity in which it is found, but also for its fine quality. This pottery is of two kinds—the wheel-turned wares of Mediterranean inspiration, which were made by the men, and the hand-molded wares of the women. The latter is uniquely African. Similar pottery is still made today—in the same distinctive styles and techniques—in many different parts of Africa, including the West—ancestral home of American Negroes.

If Kush, both at Napata and at Meroë, was important in its own right, it also holds a special significance in regard to the West African peoples who were the main contributors to the Atlantic slave trade. Kush undoubtedly spread its own distinctive influence far and wide, but it was, in addition, the main channel through which Egyptian beliefs, symbols, and technology were filtered through to Africa south of the Sahara.

And what of the West African folk? What had become of the Saharan peoples who had emigrated to the Niger River Valley in search of sustenance? All during the centuries of Egyptian and Kushite growth, Africans on the Atlantic coast were also developing their own brand of civilization—sometimes different from that of the Nile Valley, sometimes similar. Agriculture was discovered independently along the Upper Niger River in the west at about the same time that it reached the Nile Valley from Asia (5000 to 4000 B.C.). By the second millennium B.C., when Kush and Axum in the east were establishing states on the Egyptian model, the West African societies were evolving their own forms of social and political organization. Throughout the western savanna south of the Sahara there was a simultaneous rise of despotic states of purely African type, as well as the development of trade and technology. Undoubtedly some of the techniques and ideas of the western states were borrowed outright, though some of these were first adapted to local needs and preferences; others were entirely original.

Undoubtedly also, there were two main routes by which the borrowed ideas reached the west after the original diffusion of peoples and ideas from the fertile Sahara. The first route was certainly the one that led from Meroë on the Nile, for Meroë occupied a unique and important geographical position. Linked by the Nile with Mediterranean cultures, it also lay close to the caravan routes along the Atbara River leading to the Abyssinian highlands and thence to the western ports of the Indian Ocean, where Kush had long been an established trader. Furthermore, Meroë lay at the eastern borders of that vast grassland area that stretches below the Sahara from the hills of modern Ethiopia to the Atlantic Ocean. This *Sudan*, or savanna, as it is called, was named *Bilad es Sudan,* or "Land of the Blacks," by the Arabs, and for centuries caravans toiled back and forth across it between the Nile and the Niger. These trails led from Meroë through the hills of Kordofan to such settlements as Jebel Uri and Ain Fara, in Darfur, then past Lake Chad's early civilizations of the Sao and the Kotoko and the later empires of Kanem-Bornu. Beyond Lake Chad the caravans entered the great states of the Western Sudan—the lands of the Hausa states, and Ghana, Mali, and Songhai. They brought the products and ideas of the Nile Valley and the Orient and carried back in exchange those of the Western Sudan.

The second route lay across the Sahara itself from the shores of the Mediterranean. African rock art has left us visual evidence that at least two chariot routes led from North Africa to the neighborhood of Gao on the Niger, during the first millennium B.C. Later, when horses were no longer practical on the desert, camel caravans continued to cross from oasis to oasis and carried both ideas and goods from north to south and back. At least four of these caravan routes occupy positions of historical importance; the Selima Trail in the east, the Bilma and Gadames Trails to Lake Chad and Kano, and the Taodeni Trail to Timbuktu and Djenne in the Middle Niger Region.

There is certainly overwhelming evidence that many unities of thought, technique, and pattern existed between the ancient peoples of the Nile Valley and the West African folk from whom Afro-Americans sprang. And whether it be similarities in methods of ironworking, the concept of the Divine Kingship and the Queen-Sister, or the use of certain symbolic designs, we can reasonably assume that either they traveled across the continent by these ancient caravan routes as people migrated and traded across the Sudan and the Sahara, or else they arose from a common origin in the fertile Sahara.

By which of these routes iron technology reached the shore of the Atlantic is not clear. Some believe it came via Meroë; others say it traveled south across the desert from ancient Carthage. Possibly, even probably, the knowledge reached West Africa from several directions, or it may have evolved there independently, as did agriculture.

Terra-cotta Head, Nok Culture (900 B.C.–200 A.D.). (Courtesy Nigerian Museum, Lagos, Nigeria)

25

Bronze portrait head from ancient Ife, 960–1160 A.D. Executed by the lost-wax process. The longitudinal lines may indicate facial scarifications. (Courtesy Nigerian Museum, Lagos, Nigeria)

In any case, we do know that soon after 600 B.C. West Africa entered its own Iron Age—that is, it began to smelt ore and make its own iron implements. Proof of this came to light recently (1931–44) through excavations at Nok, at the confluence of the Niger and Benue rivers in central Nigeria. Radiocarbon-dating tests have established that this Nok Culture, as it is called, flourished between 300 B.C. and 200 A.D. and marked the transition from Stone Age to Iron Age. Archaeologists have disclosed not only evidence of iron-working, but a number of skillfully modeled heads in terra-cotta (baked clay).

It was the development of iron technology that, perhaps more than anything else, shaped the course of history in West Africa. The effects of the Iron Age were like a stone cast into water, spreading in ever-widening rings of influence. First came improved food production and population explosion, then expansion and organization because of improved tools and weapons for conquering man's enemies—both human and natural. Without iron there could not have developed the complex cultures that gave rise to the famous African art that reached its zenith in West Africa.

This art was closely tied in with religious and social customs, or with the "divine king," who sat godlike on the thrones of many West African states, such as Dahomey, Benin, or Kongo. These religious and social customs, and the opulent courts that patronized the arts, would not have been possible without the wealth and power that arose from iron technology.

The earliest of the great West African states of which we have any firsthand knowledge appears to have been known as *Aoukar,* though sometimes it was called after the name of its capital, *Kumbi.* We know it better as Ghana. It must not be confused with the modern state of Ghana, which is much farther south, for ancient Ghana was located to the north and northwest of the Upper Niger River. Although first heard of soon after 800 A.D., Ghana was already well established by that time. Its power lasted until the Almoravid invasion from the Muslim north led to its decline and the rise of its successors in the Western Sudan, Mali, and Songhai.

Ancient Ghana owed its strength to the superiority of its iron-pointed weapons, by means of which it dominated its weaker neighbors. That this strength was something to be reckoned with we know from the Muslim writer, El Bekri, of Cordoba, Spain (eleventh century A.D.). Working from earlier firsthand reports, he wrote: "the King of Ghana can put two hundred thousand warriors in the field. . . . The King who governs them at this moment . . . Tenkamenin . . . is master of a great empire and of a power that is formidable."

But if Ghana owed its power to iron, it owed its opulence to gold and salt, for trade and tribute were the sources of the kingdom's wealth. Salt from the Sahara, scarce in the forest lands of Guinea, was exchanged in Ghana for an equal weight of gold brought there from its secret sources in the south. "The King," it was said, "exacts the right of one dinar of gold on each donkey load of salt that goes out." This taxation in turn supported the luxury of the court, and the profitable trade brought affluence to its merchants. Both encouraged and patronized the fine craftsmen for which Ghana was famed.

El Bekri has described the pomp and majesty of the Ghanaian court as follows: "When the king gives an audience to his people, to listen to their complaints and to set them to rights, he sits in a pavilion around which stand ten pages holding shields and gold-mounted swords. On his right hand are the sons of the princes of his empire, splendidly clad and with gold plaited in their hair. The governor of the city is seated on the ground in front of the king, and all around him are his counselors in the same position. . . . The gate of the chamber is guarded by dogs . . . [that] wear collars of gold and silver, ornamented with metals. . . ."

26

The rulers of Ghana shrewdly maintained the value of gold, as El Bekri made clear. "All nuggets of gold that are found in the mines of this empire," he said, "belong to the king; but he leaves to his people the gold dust that everyone knows. Without this precaution gold would become so plentiful that it would practically lose its value."

Nor was Ghana the exception in Black Africa. Mali and Songhai succeeded it as dominant trading states in the Western Sudan, and such Muslim writers as Ibn Batuta and Ibn Khaldun (fourteenth century) have described their opulence with the same enthusiasm El Bekri had for Ghana. These two states came under the influence of Islam and the fabled journey to Mecca made by Mali's king, Mansa Kankan Musa, is still spoken of with awe because of the extravagant luxury of his caravan.

The pomp and splendor of these courts encouraged further development of the applied arts and crafts and the evolution of sophisticated techniques such as *cire-perdue* (lost wax), brass-casting, filigree work, and embossing. The voluminous and elaborate clothes adopted by the people of these kingdoms encouraged the art of weaving in silk, wool, and cotton. The latter, especially, was a valuable item of export. Leatherworking, pottery- or jewelry-making, and the use of baked clay for architecture became highly skilled arts in the Western Sudan. However, the tabus of Islam prevented the development of the splendid figure sculpture that came from the pagan religions of West Africa and the courts of its divine kings.

These pagan kingdoms, like those of the Islamized Sudan, had risen and fallen all during the centuries preceding the advent of the first Europeans to the West African coast in the mid-fifteenth century. We know of their history primarily through hearsay and oral traditions, for archaeological research has been limited in this region and written records are virtually nonexistent. One important archaeological discovery, however, was made in a series of excavations begun in 1910 at Ife, in Nigeria. A number of strikingly beautiful portrait heads done in terra-cotta and in bronze were unearthed there. The bronze heads were cast by the sophisticated and difficult *cire-perdue* technique and appear to represent members of the royal family and court. Carbon dating places them between the tenth and eighteenth centuries, with the best work belonging to the earlier dates.

Although the early history of these peoples of West Africa is still obscure, it is certain that at least by the thirteenth century a number of states and empires, which were similar in pattern to those of the Sudan, had emerged along the Atlantic coast.

Until the fifteenth century, Europe had been receiving African goods from the rich lands of Guinea via the Sudanic trade routes across the Sahara to the Mediterranean. But in 1441 the Portuguese, in search of a way to avoid the North African middlemen, first landed on the west coast of Africa, near Cape Verde. By 1471 they had reached the Gold Coast, which they found so rich in gold that in 1482 they set up a fort at *Elmina* (The Mine) in order to monopolize the trade with the local rulers. The latter much impressed the Europeans with their fine manners and elegant protocol.

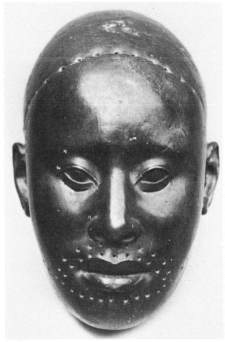

Bronze head from ancient Ife. It is thought to represent the Oni Obalufon II. The holes around the mouth and hairline were either for ritual bead pendants or for human or animal hair. (Courtesy, Nigerian Museum, Lagos, Nigeria)

Terra-cotta head from ancient Ife. Note longitudinal lines similar to those on bronze heads. (Courtesy, Nigerian Museum, Lagos, Nigeria)

Bronze female head from the altar of the Queen Mother of Benin. The latticework pattern of the hairdress is similar to those worn by the Obas (Kings) of Benin as an emblem of authority. Note the three Bini tribal marks over each eye. (Courtesy, University Museum)

At about the same time, the first Portuguese explorers arrived at the mouth of the Congo River and found there the large and thriving Kingdom of Kongo, which controlled an area about the size of California. Its royal court was located at the capital city of Mbanzakongo, and it had an aristocracy of governors, chiefs, and functionaries, as well as an efficient system of taxation.

The king, or *Manikongo,* was described by a European traveler as follows:

The King of Kongo, when hee goeth to the Campe to see his Armie, rideth upon an Elephant in great pompe and majestie. On either side of the Elephant he hath six slaves two of them were Kings, that he himselfe had taken in the field . . . Then there followeth a More [Moor] which doth nothing but talke aloud in praise of the King, telling what a great warriour he hath been and praising his wisdom for all things that he hath accomplished. . . .

The Portuguese had no difficulty in setting up trade and diplomatic relations with this kingdom, and very early they made trading contacts with other states on its perimeter, such as Loango, Matamba, and Ndongo. (The chief of Ndongo held the hereditary title of *Ngola,* from which came the name of the later Portuguese colony of Angola and the term "Gullah," applied to certain Negroes in South Carolina.) Farther inland were the great kingdoms of the Luba-Lunda and the Bashi-Bushongo.

Here, in the southwestern savanna where the raphia palm grows, the Congolese people have traditionally made exquisite, velvet-like pile cloth from its fibers. This raphia cloth, ivory, hides, and slaves formed the main items of trade with the Portuguese. The Kongo also maintained a royal fishery at Luanda, where *azimbu,* or shells used for money, were obtained.

All of this vastly changed the course of history in Africa, for now the Saharan traffic to the Sudan was outflanked, as European ships sailed around the western hump of Africa and set up trading posts all along the Atlantic coast between Cape Verde and the southern desert. This development led to the slow decline of Sudanic states, such as Mali, and to the gradual emergence of several new ones along the coastal fringes of the forest lands to their south.

The nuclei for these polities were already there, and some had been long established. This was, after all, the southern end of the salt-gold trading routes that had brought prosperity to Ghana, Mali, and Songhai. But the scramble for this new Atlantic trade—first in goods and later in slaves—created new political tensions, and new kingdoms arose on the scene.

Between the Senegal and Gambia rivers, in the region known as the Senegambia, the important empire of the Wolofs held sway. South of that the Mandingos remained dominant. Just west of the Volta River lived the great Akan peoples, whose early states of Bobo and Banda were finally succeeded by the Kingdom of the Ashanti, which rapidly became the major Gold Coast power. Between the Volta and the Benue rivers, the Yoruba state of Oyo long was paramount over Benin and the rest of Yorubaland as well. Even Dahomey, perched perilously between Ashanti and Oyo rule, paid tribute to the latter until the Fon at Abomey began their bid for independence in the eighteenth century.

All these empires and kingdoms along the west coast of Africa were related linguistically and had many cultural attributes in common. In particular, the divine kingship and pagan religion inspired a great art throughout this region. Here, also, wealth and power through trade brought about both the demand and the supply of finely wrought luxury goods, through later this was self-destructive as the trade in goods gave way to the trade in men. The Atlantic slave trade substituted manufactured goods for the artistic production of expert craftsmen. Firearms and European politics created chaos, dissension, and decadence among the Africans and finally brought about the downfall of the courts that had fostered the arts and crafts. Later, European missionaries discouraged the pagan religion that had produced so much beautiful sculpture.

But until the madness of "slave fever" brought about their final disintegration, it was these West African states that shaped the culture of the black men and women who came to this country as slaves. And a predominant feature of the West African civilization was its fine craftsmanship and its capacity for a great art.

# 2 WEST AFRICAN ART AND CRAFT

Akwete cloth, which is made of cotton and sometimes rayon and silk, gets its name from the town of
Akwete in Eastern Nigeria, where it is handwoven on
looms that produce a cloth measuring 48 by 72
inches, called a "fathom." It takes a weaver about
ten days to make a fathom.

Bronze plaque showing king and attendants from Benin. Note the high coral collar still worn by the Oba of Benin. (Courtesy, The Museum of Primitive Art)

It has already been mentioned that West African art owed much to religion and to royalty. These were, in fact, closely related, since the king was considered semidivine, an emissary from heaven, a symbol of the nation's prosperity. The artist lived mainly on court patronage and supplied art objects to glorify the person and deeds of the monarch. He built imposing halls, made thrones, scepters, axes, swords, or other symbols of authority, as well as ancestor figures. Nor was personal adornment left out: handsomely woven cloth, and jewelry of every description, helped to show the riches and high position of the wearer and added to his prestige. And just as the European courtier dressed his servants in elaborate livery of silks and satins, so the African's wealth could be shown to the world by the lavish way in which he ornamented his slaves with heavy cast-brass anklets or other adornment.

We know little of the early civilization at Nok, but the magnificent bronzes of Ife were undoubtedly the result of court patronage, and one may be a portrait bust of the Oni, or king, of Ife himself. Though we know of Ife only through such artifacts or oral history, Benin, another great kingdom, has left behind more precise historical evidence of its greatness and the sophistication of its court-fostered art. Europeans, from the fifteenth century onward, have left us written records of the riches and complexities of this kingdom before it degenerated through the slave trade.

When the Portuguese first reached Benin in 1472, they found a city-state that was prosperous and greatly skilled in the working of metals and of wood. The art of bronze-casting had been introduced to Benin during the reign of Oba (king) Oguola (about the year 1280); Ighu-igha, an artist sent at that time from Ife to Benin, is still venerated by smiths today. Between that date and the arrival of the Europeans, Benin and its art flourished. In 1668, the Dutch geographer Olfert Dapper described the orderly and extensive city with its great fortifications, its neat rows of solidly built houses set out in thirty broad streets "seven times as broad as those in Holland." These dwellings had long interior galleries and courtyards, with polished clay walls that resembled marble. Some houses had small turrets on which were perched birds, made of bronze, similar to the ibis. The pomp and extravagance of the court was often described by Dapper and other travelers. The Oba's palace was said to be very great, with many square courtyards in each of which a watch was kept. The palace apartments had galleries "as big as those on the Exchange at Amsterdam," and were supported by "wooden pillars encased with copper where their victories are depicted." The king received his visitors graciously in the presence of his great counselors. He was seated on an ivory throne under a canopy of Indian silk. The copper, or bronze, plaques mentioned here were removed from the pillars by the time the British punitive expedition arrived in 1897 to destroy the city, but many of them still survive in the world's great art galleries.

Though the Ashanti and Dahomean courts were of much later inception, they too followed the pattern of the earlier kingdoms in their opulence and the semidivinity of their kings. Dalzell's *History of Dahomey* (1793) is illustrated with plates of the king's court at his capital of Abomey. He is pictured being fanned by his slaves and protected from the heat of the sun by fanciful umbrellas, or shaded by an elaborate silken pavilion. He is surrounded by his courtiers and his famous "Amazons," or soldier-wives, elegantly attired in gowns and jewelry, their turbans topped by ostrich plumes. In the capital city, skilled craftsmen produced the beautiful appliqué wall hangings that were the royal prerogative.

The Ashanti also reserved one fabric for their rulers. The exquisite Kente cloth, woven of gold and silken fibers, was proscribed for the commonality. Each rectangular pattern in its design carried a message, such as "long life," "happiness," "wealth," "justice," and the like, and could thus be used to glorify the special attributes of the wearer. Silk material from other countries was meticulously raveled by the Akan people of Ashanti, and rewoven into the Kente cloth designs.

Even at the courts, however, where the king was often equated with a particular god or regarded as a special emissary from heaven, he frequently represented the "spirit" of the tribe as well, and the ceremonial regalia was tied in with religion in a complex way. To a tribal African, life is synonymous with religious living. He believes in one Supreme Being, although he does not visualize this Being as a man, but rather as a soul-force or energy manifesting itself in all life. This belief, together with ancestor-worship and the idea of the divine kingship, are so intricately interwoven that it is impossible to draw a hard-and-fast line between religious and secular purposes.

The "Golden Stool" of the Ashanti is a case in point. Until about 1700 the Akan clans and family groups had merely recognized a loose relationship with one another, but they stood apart. Then two great leaders, Okomfo Enokye and Osei Tuto, arose and forged the Ashanti union, a political alliance strong enough to withstand its enemies, and the "Golden Stool" became symbolic of that union. According to legend, as retold in W.E.F. Ward's *History of Ghana* (1958):

> One Friday a great gathering was held at Kumasi; and there Enokye brought down from the sky, with darkness and thunder, and in a thick cloud of white dust, a wooden stool adorned with gold, which floated to earth and alighted gently on Osei Tuto's knees. This stool, Enokye announced, contained the spirit of the whole Ashanti nation, and all its strength and bravery depended on the safety of the stool. . . .

Thus, the stool served a secular purpose in maintaining the unity of the state, but it was also worshiped as the spirit of the Ashanti nation. At the death of the king, or *Asantahene,* the stool was blackened and placed in the stool house and dedicated to his memory. A beautiful object in itself, carved with an adze from a single piece of wood and covered with sheets of gold, it was both a work of art and an example of fine craftsmanship; it served god, king, and nation as well.

It is this ritualistic use of art in Africa that helps us to reconstruct the world left behind by the African slave shipped to America. For the ritual object had to meet rigorously applied standards established by generations of use; in spite of a wide latitude of variation permitted the individual artist, most African art was governed by rigid traditions, many of which have persisted to this day. Therefore, by studying the arts and crafts of twentieth-century Africa, and what few antiquities remain, we can know something of West African art and crafts during the slaving period.

Mention has already been made of entire villages that acquired reputations for excellence in one or another of the crafts. It was much more common, however, for specialization to take place within the community itself. Many of the crafts were restricted to certain families and to organized guilds. Skills were transmitted by an apprentice system to a son or daughter or another blood relative. It was possible, but much more difficult, for someone outside the family to arrange for apprenticeship. The guilds, like those in Europe,

Kente cloth, fabric traditionally reserved for Ashanti chiefs. The narrow strips were woven by men and then sewn together to make a wider piece. Colors were traditionally red, green, and white, combined with gold thread. (Collection Old Slave Mart Museum. Photo, author)

Akwete cloth. The variety of the traditional designs used in these textiles is wide, but they are generally restricted to geometrical patterns.

Mpongwe mask. Wood. Many Gabon tribes produce similar masks. The coastal area of the Mpongwe is merely the place where they are sold to Europeans, so they have come to be known as "Mpongwe style." Africans often paint their masks white because this color is symbolic of the spirit world.

Shene-Malula mask. Bakuba. An example of the way in which Africans often combine many materials in one art form. Carved of wood, the mask is decorated with paint, cowrie shells, and beads, and is topped by a hat of woven vegetable fibers.

helped perpetuate the skills and traditions, and also maintained high standards of quality.

Social stratification related to a man's occupation developed quite early in Africa. While the particular social order varied from tribe to tribe, there was a widespread custom of dignifying or degrading families on the basis of their occupations. This fact becomes particularly relevant when we come to consider the Negro in the New World, as will be seen later. Work in itself did not affect a family's status, but the nature of the work did.

There were, in general, three types of handcrafts. Many articles of common use could be made by any person willing to try, though some were by tradition made by men and others by women. At the other extreme were those sacred things the making of which was kept secret. In between were many articles that had to be made by certain families or guilds. Yet there was occasional overlapping. A smith, for instance, might be the head of the local secret society and thus be authorized to make sacred articles for secret rituals. At the same time, he could and did make hoes, spears, or other articles of everyday use for individuals.

Thus, each object fell into one of several categories: those connected with public ceremonies of a social or religious nature, articles of trade, and those for the private use of the individual. The latter included objects such as amulets, fetishes, or ancestor figures that were related to religious beliefs, as well as mundane articles such as tools or cooking utensils.

With few exceptions, the Negroes of West Africa have always viewed the ironworker with respect, a mixture of fear and honor. Because his skills were needed to fashion various cult objects, he was necessarily a member of the secret societies and was privy to all important decisions made by the cult in controlling the tribal community. In addition, because of his contact with fire, magic powers were often ascribed to him. Thus, through these twin elements of the sacred and secular, he often combined the functions of medicine man, chief, and maker of magic figures. A religious aura surrounded his work and a certain mythology, born of awe of the fire and the molten metal, enveloped the process of ironmaking. To the African, the forging of metal was a poetic and mystical experience, a creative process by which metal, through fire, became infused with life. It was also a fearsome process. To the Yoruba, *Ogun,* the deity of smithing, was a double spirit of creativity and destructiveness, since fire can destroy as well as create.

The smelting of iron, although known in Africa from the first millennium B.C., remained a rather simple process, with little change over the centuries. One reason for this is that Africans discovered early that, instead of laboriously processing the metal themselves, imported iron could be obtained more easily from Europeans in exchange for articles that were abundant and easy to come by—including human slaves. In fact, the Slatees, or African slave merchants, priced their human chattel as so many "bars of iron." A bar equalled two shillings, and a slave was worth £15, or 150 bars.

Because the work of the smith was much more highly skilled than that of the smelter, it was not so easily replaced by European substitutes, and the smith retained his special place in African society. Smiths belonged to such powerful guilds that they often crossed tribal lines. In northern Liberia, for instance, when a smith was taken prisoner-of-war, he was set free if he could prove he really was a smith by forging whatever was designated by his captors. The customs pertaining to the smith in Liberia are generally typical throughout West Africa.

According to Harley and Schwab's 1947 report of the Peabody Museum's expedition to Liberia in 1928, many of the smith's mysteries were kept secret or semisecret, especially from women, who were never allowed into a smithy. In some cases, screens of raffia were built around the forge so that women could not even take a secret peek. Its processes were hedged in by all sorts of ceremonies and tabus, many of which were sexual, no doubt because of the creative connotations of the work. Bellows often were decorated with phallic symbols; smiths or smelters were required to abstain from sexual intercourse and could not even look at their wives before work for fear the work would not go properly. They were pragmatic enough, however, to provide for human frailty, and counter-medicine was provided for use when these stringent tabus were not adhered to!

Although the smithy was always popular as a gathering place for men to exchange news and gossip, everyone was required strictly to observe all its tabus. Some of these affected actions, as did the tabu that forbade walking behind the smith when he was working hot iron; others pertained to objects, as did the Mano tabus against bringing rice fanners or bows and arrows into the forge, for fear the softness of one or the brittleness of the other would make the iron soft or brittle by sympathetic magic. In some cases, the smith's strong "medicine" extended to those around him, as, for instance, when anyone hard-pressed by the law, even for murder, could take sanctuary in the smithy, much as Christians can in a church.

While some metal objects were handwrought on an anvil, Africans also excelled at the casting of metal. Bronze and other alloys used in the kingdoms of the Guinea coast contain little tin and more zinc and lead, and are sometimes referred to as "cast brass." There were two methods of casting: solid casting, a process in which the mold is scooped out of wet clay or sand, and the more complicated technique known as *cire-perdue,* or lost wax, which is described in detail below. It was by the latter process that the finest works of art were formed. Embossing, engraving, hammering, inlaying of metal and other materials, damascening of copper and brass, and the intricate use of braided wire were among other techniques practiced.

Artistry in the working of metals varied from tribe to tribe and period to period. The bronzes of Ife and Benin are both superior in their earlier examples, but they tended to degenerate in later periods. Most African art is stylized and symbolic, rather than realistic, but the Ife heads are an exception. The obvious talent for lifelike portraiture possessed by the artists of Ife reminds us that a similar naturalism was introduced into Egyptian art by the Kushitic Twenty-fifth Dynasty. Although Benin produced some beautiful representational pieces, such as the female head from the altar of the Queen Mother of Benin, others are highly stylized. Both are equally beautiful, though different.

The Ife heads and the Benin bronzes, as well as many other examples of West African art, were done by the difficult and sophisticated *cire-perdue* process. First the figure is molded in wax, frequently around a core of clay, and small details of ornamentation are carefully modeled. On this wax mold a coating of clay is applied; when the clay is heated, the wax runs out (or is "lost"), thus leaving an opening between inner and outer clay core into which the molten metal is poured. Since the clay core is finally broken up (i.e., "lost form"), there is no margin for error. The piece must be perfect the first time, or the whole process must be repeated. After removal from the mold, finishing touches are put on by polishing, engraving, etc.

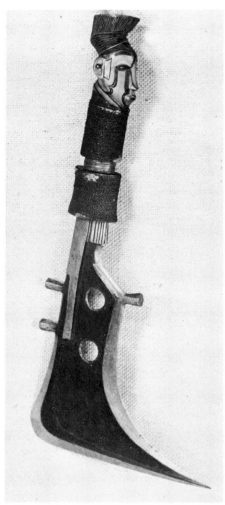

Ceremonial ax, part of a Mangbetu bride's dowry. A beautiful example of the African smith's art. (Although the Mangbetu were not within the slavers' range, such fine metalwork was widespread in West Africa. Detail of ax shows the beautifully carved wood head. In Africa several arts are often combined in one article in this fashion. (Collection Old Slave Mart Museum. Photos, author)

Three anklets typical of the fine cast brass made by the Dan-Ngere tribes of Liberia. The heavy shackle rings are the emblem worn by the chief's wife. (Collection Old Slave Mart Museum. Photo, author)

Besides the pieces made for elaborate courts such as Benin, many other types of metalwork were executed by Africans. The Ibo smiths (in what is now Nigeria) produced beautiful iron gates known as the Awka gates. The individual African had to come to the smith to obtain tools and implements of all kinds. Armorers of several tribes were highly skilled in the forging of weapons both for ceremonial use as well as hunting or war. Brass, bronze, iron, or copper anklets and bracelets were popular forms of ornamentation and in some cases served to show the status of the wearer as well. Some were produced by casting and others were forged.

Silver in West Africa was mainly worked into jewelry, especially in Islamic countries, where gold had been prohibited by the Prophet. The silver was obtained primarily from melted-down coins.

Gold, on the other hand, was once plentiful; it was the main source of wealth in ancient days. The king of ancient Ghana, as we have seen, monopolized the worthwhile pieces so as to control the market, and Ghana's prosperity depended on the gold-salt trade.

Ashanti weight in the form of a body lying beneath a king's stool, which represents the *Kra* or soul of the Ashanti nation. See page 33. (Collection Old Slave Mart Museum. Photo, author)

We have no way of knowing what the work of ancient Ghana's goldsmiths was like, since none of her antiquities have been found, but we do know something of that "Gold Coast" farther south, which was the source of Ghana's gold. This was Ashanti-land, in what is now Ghana. Little remains of the fabulous gold ornaments of the kings of Ashanti, however. Since gold was used primarily as a medium of exchange, little attention was paid to its artistic value, so gold objects were melted down again and again. But, as a by-product of the extensive gold trade, we have been left with many exquisite small gold weights of cast brass made by the Ashanti. These beautiful pieces were cast by the lost-wax process in the form of birds, fish, men, and women, or merely small ornamented squares. Used in the measuring of gold dust, they are remarkable for the accuracy of their weight as well as the perfection of their design. The Ashanti weights are interesting not only for their technical skill but also for their symbolism. Although some were actually used for weighing gold dust, others seem to have served more as status symbols, ornaments, charms, or fetishes. All Ashanti gold belonged to the king, who represented the nation, though commoners could hold it in trust and use it in trade. The symbolism of the weights constantly reminded the people of the omnipresence and omnipotence of the divinity from whom the king derived his authority.

Gold thread was woven by the Ashanti into the royal Kente cloth worn by its rulers. Breastplates, hilts and sheaths of weapons, finger, wrist, and knee bracelets, as well as small figures and masks were finely wrought of gold by the Ashanti. The magnificent gold mask of King Kofi is one of the most spectacular pieces to have survived as evidence of all this splendor.

In addition to the usual symbolism connected with the forging of other metals, gold and silver held special connotations for the African. To the Ashanti, gold was synonymous with both the sun and the king, reflecting the light and life of the nation. Silver, the color of moonlight, represented the queen and the moon as well.

More ubiquitous than metals in the art-producing regions of West Africa was wood. There were the hardwoods of the forests and the soft, lighter woods of the savanna. Local carvers each had their own preferences. The most frequently used were the bombax tree and other woods similar to ebony and mahogany. These were utilized in building houses and were combined with either dried clay or thatch; they were made into drums, food vessels, stools, or headrests; logs were hollowed out into canoes or grain mortars and carved into doors. But wood was used principally for the carving of ancestor

African drums. Foreground, two small Bashi drums. Rear left. Watutsi; right, Bakuba. Only the latter tribe lay within the slaving range. Note the beautiful incised decoration. (Collection Old Slave Mart Museum. Photo, author)

Bakwele mask. The characteristic heart shape with the strong vertical nose ridge supporting the brows delights African sculptors of the Fang, Bakota, Bakwele, and Balaga tribes. (Collection Old Slave Mart Museum, Photo, author)

figures, fetishes, or masks. The latter served to give anonymity to the officials wearing them and thus to dignify the office, just as police or military uniforms do in America or justices' wigs do in Great Britain. The masks were both works of art and instruments of social control.

Because of his role in making ritualistic objects, the wood-sculptor was almost as important as the smith in the hierarchy of craftsmen. At court the woodcarver reached the highest rank, but he was well respected in all African society. If a young man wanted to become a carver, he might serve an apprenticeship to a well-known carver, much as was done in the smiths' guilds. The master carver was paid with gifts, both during and after the apprenticeship. Not only did the initiate learn the technique of carving, but he had to learn also what rules to observe, for certain principles were prescribed by the traditions and concepts of the entire community for generations. Within these limitations, however, there was still scope for imagination and individuality. The sculptor managed to add a personal note of his own while adhering to the rules laid down for him.

The woodcarver was a highly trained craftsman in every sense of the word. He knew so thoroughly the characteristics of his woods, the use of his tools, and the various tribal styles that his carving became automatic and instinctive. He followed the rules without thinking about them, which freed him to express himself creatively within these confines. This is why we can so easily recognize a particular mask or fetish as belonging to a certain tribe or cult, even though no two pieces are exactly alike.

Wood, to many Africans, is not dead matter. It is still alive all through the carving process; cutting and chopping it causes it pain, and the spirit of the tree must be asked forgiveness. This is one reason we come across so many rites in connection with the carving of wood. Another is that wood is so often used for cult objects, the creation of which is an extremely sacred act. Before beginning work the woodcarver undergoes some kind of ritual cleansing, refraining from all pleasure, as does the smith, and then devotes himself to his work in seclusion.

Unlike the European or American woodcarver, the Afro-American's ancestor preferred to use the adze, rather than the knife, as his principal tool, and he handled it with the utmost precision. The piece was first roughed out with bold, hacking blows of a large adze, then completed with a smaller one. Piercing or removal of material from beneath arms and legs was often aided by burning it out with a hot iron. The piece was lovingly finished in a variety of ways. Some artists polished their work with soot or grease. Another traditional method was to treat the wood with sap from roots and leaves, or with fine camwood powder *(tukula).* (The latter was a protection against termites, which are one of the worst threats to African art. Their depredations make it almost impossible to find genuine African antiquities made of wood.) Use also added its own patina as the object was smoothed by handling, blackened with the smoke and dust from the hut, or sprinkled with libations of beer or blood, which gave the wood its characteristic bronze color.

Unlike most sculpture in Western art, much of African sculpture is decorated, especially the masks. Paint is more likely to be found on masks than on figures, and then only in the symbolic colors of red, black, or white. But other materials are generously used: natural hair, ivory inlays, skin, animals' tusks, horns, fabric and feathers, beads, nails, and seashells are all utilized, more to honor the figures themselves than to delight the viewers. Burned and incised patterns are often employed. Cowrie shells appear with particular frequency on cult objects because of their resemblance to female genitalia, which gives them significance as a fertility symbol.

Two versions of the mask worn by the High Priestess of the Bundu Society, Sierra Leone. They illustrate the individuality expressed by the African carvers within prescribed forms. All Bundu masks have the high domed forehead, the helmet-like hairdress, and the rolls of fat around the neck, signifying corpulence — and thus beauty. (Left, photo I.F.A.N., Dakar, Senegal. Above, loan by Mrs. Warren Whatley, Jr.)

A fine example of a male Tji-Wara (antelope), Bambara. The female is always represented with young on her back. Dancers wearing fiber costumes and red face masks, and crowned by these carvings that often rise to 32 inches or more, perform fertility dances in pairs imitating the great leaps of the antelope. (Courtesy, Museum of Primitive Art)

Ashanti Akua 'mma, fertility dolls carried by young girls to influence their unborn children. The stylized one on the right is more traditional. Those on the left are evolved types. (Collection Old Slave Mart Museum. Photo, author)

All African wood sculpture is generally static and symmetrical, and the contours of the tree trunk can usually be seen. However, some is more naturalistic and some more conventionalized or cubist in feeling. The two styles cannot be ascribed to any one racial or environmental influence—Islamic, matriarchal or patriarchal, etc.—since both are found together in the same tribe, or sometimes even in the same statue. But because most African art serves a ceremonial and/or religious purpose, we are apt to find it simplified, conventionalized, or with certain elements grossly exaggerated to emphasize their intended use. Symbolism naturally plays a large part. Fertility (both human and agricultural) is expressed by large heads, huge breasts, or prominent sexual organs. Power is implied by the introduction of certain animals thought to have this characteristic; horns of buffaloes, rams, and antelopes, or the snouts of crocodiles all serve this purpose.

The African sculptor also used soft stone for carving in some localities, notably the borderlands of Sierra Leone and Liberia as well as the Lower Congo and Yorubaland. There is a splendid stone rams' head housed in the museum of Ife (Nigeria), and some interesting monoliths and figure carvings have been found both in the forests of Nigeria as well as in Angola. At Esie, about 60 miles north of Ife, some 800 fragmentary stone figures have been discovered. They may date back to the eighteenth-century kingdom of Nupe. The Ekoi, on the Upper Cross River in southeast Nigeria, have left some monolithic ancestor figures, also in stone. Oral tradition says that they are very ancient, though they may actually date from a much later period. Small soapstone figures are now used by the Mende of Sierra Leone and the Kissi of Guinea as rice gods to bring a rich harvest. They were found buried in the ground and are probably relics of a much earlier civilization. Called *nomoli*, they are characterized by disproportionately large heads and bulging eyes. They are carved as a sculptural mass. Occasionally, other pieces of stone sculpture may be found among the Bakongo or the Baluba of the Congo. And in the Noqui Massif in Angola there are some statues made of steatite, called *mintadi*, which are regarded as guardians of graves. Some of these date back to about the seventeenth century.

Ivory, both elephant and the less fine hippo ivory, was initially valued as a symbol of power. It was worked by several tribes—surprisingly well, considering the tools used. Sometimes real masterpieces were produced, as in the case of the elaborately carved elephant tusks kept in the royal shrines of ancient Benin. Amulets, handles, jewelry, and other objects were made of ivory or bone. The horns of animals served many purposes and were meticulously carved into animal or bird shapes.

The art of basketry was another important craft in West Africa, because the appropriate raw materials were plentiful, and it reached a high degree of excellence there. Natural fibers were, in fact, second only to wood as a versatile material. Sisal-like plants, palms, reeds, and creepers from the forest were all put to use, after being treated in various ways. They were dried, split, or soaked to make them more pliable, and then woven into many different kinds of useful articles.

As a rule this was woman's work, and girls learned the craft from their mothers while very young. In some localities the men also did some basketry, especially during the dry season when there was no work in the fields.

Various techniques were employed. In coiling, the most popular method in West Africa, a core of one or more materials was coiled round and round continuously upon itself. The successive coils were sewn together firmly with a thin, flexible fiber such as raffia or split palm fronds. Checkerwork and

Baluba funerary mask, talc stone. This mask is placed on a tomb to guard the spirit of the deceased. (Collection Old Slave Mart Museum, Photo, author)

Metal *minyaki*. This displays characteristics of the western Bapende: arched eyebrows joined above the retroussé nose, bulging forehead, plaited headdress, prominent nostrils and heavy triangular eyelids, as well as broad, high cheekbones, and pointed chin. (Collection Old Slave Mart Museum, Photo, author)

Ivory amulets, Bapende. When made of ivory, these miniature masks called *minyaki* are reserved for initiates, to signify they have gone through the *kimpasi* ritual, the test for admission to adult society. These amulets are all about 1½ inches, actual size. (Collection Old Slave Mart Museum. Photo, author)

41

Musical instruments. A very old raft zither (rear) with vegetable fiber strings. In front are "finger pianos" (*sansa, ikelembe,* or *mbira*). Usually strips of metal of varying lengths are run over and under braces, and the pitch of each "key" can be changed by sliding the metal in and out to alter its length, producing a soft, attractive sound not unlike a harp. (Collection Old Slave Mart Museum. Photo, author)

Liberian baskets: top, black and white twilled rice fanner, similar in shape to those made by Afro-Americans in South Carolina; right, black and white diagonally twilled matting holder; center, oval wickerwork hamper, diagonal weave. (Collection Old Slave Mart Museum. Photo, author)

Fine bias-weave raffia bag, made by women of the Gbunde or Loma tribes, Liberia. (Collection Old Slave Mart Museum. Photo, author)

Flour sifter from Liberia, side and bottom views. Soft and flexible, the basket is held between the hands and gently pressed while it is rotated back and forth, thus shaking the cassava flour out between the fibers. Many African baskets utilize several techniques in the same article, as this one does. The top is checkerwork, the sides twined, and the bottom twilled. (Collection Old Slave Mart Museum. Photo, author)

Cone-shaped Liberian dip-net of cord from oil-palm fiber; when in use, its circumference is fastened to a rigid hoop of vine. The calabash, an African gourd, is used as a vessel; designs are scratched, burned, or incised in the rind. Detail of net shows how the fibers are merely twisted together, a transition from basketry to true netting. (Collection Old Slave Mart Museum. Photos, author)

twilling were similar, both having warp and weft of the same size, thickness, and pliability, and varying only in the order of weaving. For a twined basket, the weft was normally not a single element but consisted of two or more strands, twisted or braided around successive warps and passed alternately over and under these. Wickerwork was also popular; it consisted of an inflexible warp and flexible weft, which passed over and under one warp at a time.

Matting was made with or without a loom, in the manner of baskets, and could be either twilled or twined. Sometimes the men employed a simple loom to make a mat in which the weft was not continuous, with each strip sticking out at the sides in a sort of fringe. A heavier mat was made of perforated reed. Parallel rows of reeds were punctured at intervals with a long, thin matting needle and closely strung on cords passing through the holes.

The women of the Gbunde and Loma tribes in Liberia made a delicate raffia bag in a bias weave. Woven without shuttle or beater, the threads were pressed home with the fingers, yet the bags were sometimes so closely woven that they were waterproof. The weaving was started on the ground, then tied to a post—or bottom-side up to a roof rafter—and held taut by the worker. After the bag was completed, the loose ends were plaited and tied.

Baskets, bowls, sifters, fanners for winnowing grain, fish traps, boxes, shields, and quivers, as well as cushions or mats to hang on wall or sit on, were all made by these various techniques. Costumes for ceremonies, hats, and jewelry, as well as strings for musical instruments, were also made of vegetable fibers.

Netting was related to basketry, but it was never woven. In weaving, the intersecting strands simply crossed each other. In netting, the threads forming the mesh were held in place by knots made with the aid of a netting needle. The space between the knots was measured and kept even with a mesh gauge (usually a rectangular piece of wood or bone). Various types of knots were used.

Another technique was sometimes used to make flexible bags or fishnets in which the intersecting strands were simply twisted together rather than knotted. It was thus a transition from basket-weaving to true netting.

Sometimes the beauty of the interlacing design was thought to be sufficient pattern, but black and uncolored materials were often alternated, and occasionally dyes of various colors were introduced, or decorations of colored wool, leather, or cowrie shells were added.

Another craft that was practiced throughout West Africa was the weaving of textiles. Although European cloth was highly prized as trade goods and slaves were often priced in terms of so many "pieces of India" (i.e., lengths of cotton cloth), the West Africans were expert weavers in their own right and sold blue homespun to the "Moors," according to the English explorer, Mungo Park. The process has changed little since Park's *Travels in the Interior Districts of Africa,* which he wrote in 1797; he described weaving in the Western Sudan as follows:

The women are very diligent in manufacturing cotton cloth. They prepare the cotton for spinning, by laying it in small quantities at the time upon a smooth stone, or piece of wood, and rolling the seeds out with a thick iron spindle, and they spin it with the distaff: The thread is not fine, but well twisted, and makes a very durable cloth. A woman with common diligence will spin from six to nine garments of this cloth in one year. . . . The weaving is performed by the men: The loom is made exactly upon the same principle

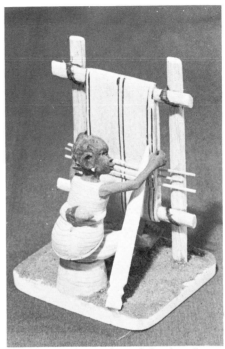

Contemporary African carving made from large thorns, illustrating the type of vertical loom operated by women. Carving is by Lamuren, Shagamu, Liberia. (Collection Old Slave Mart Museum, Photo, author)

Weaver with horizontal loom in Dakar, Senegal. The foot-operated treadle controls the heddles or harnesses above. The more harnesses there are, the greater variation of pattern permitted. These looms produce long, narrow strips. (Photo, author)

Predyed, woven-in *Okene* cloth, Nigeria. Cloths are named after the town in which they are made, according to the local name for the cloth, or a descriptive term. (Collection Old Slave Mart Museum, Photo, author)

as that of Europe, but so small and narrow that the web is seldom more than four inches broad. The shuttle is of the common construction, but as the thread is coarse, the chamber is somewhat larger than the European.

The women dye this cloth of a rich and lasting blue colour by the following simple process; the leaves of the indigo when fresh gathered are pounded in a wooden mortar, and mixed with a strong lye of wood ashes; chamber lye is sometimes added. The cloth is steeped in this mixture, and allowed to remain until it has acquired the proper shade . . . the colour is very beautiful, with a fine purple gloss, and equal in my opinion to the best Indian or European blue. This cloth is cut into various pieces, and sewed into garments with needles of the native's own making.

That this was not considered any special skill is made apparent by Park, who goes on to say, "As the arts of weaving, dyeing, sewing, etc. may be easily acquired, those who follow it are not considered in Africa, as following any particular profession: for almost every slave can weave, and every boy can sew."

In some parts of West Africa the weaving was done by women on vertical looms, but in the Sudan, where Park explored the Upper Niger as far as Segu and Djenne, it was the men who did the work and the looms were horizontal treadle looms for weaving narrow bands, such as those described by Park above. The materials were chiefly cotton and wool. Silk is not indigenous to Africa, but, as has been mentioned, the early Ashanti used to unravel Dutch silk fabrics and reweave them according to traditionally prescribed and symbolic designs.

The symbolic use of patterns is widespread throughout Africa, in woodcarving and other forms of art as well as in weaving. Thus, a zigzag line can suggest lightning, a snake, water, fire, or the mane of an antelope; a circled dot may refer to the sun as a source of great vitality. The *adinkra* mourning garments of the Ashanti are imprinted in a design of symbolic significance. The patterns were sometimes woven in with predyed thread, or the cloth might be dyed in various ways after it was taken off the loom.

There were three principal ways in which dyes were utilized: the *direct* method, in which the fabric was printed with small stamps cut from pieces of calabash or other materials; the *corroding* method, in which the cloth was first dyed a dark color, then painted with some bleaching agent that, when washed off, left a light-colored design on a solid background; and the *resist* method, in which the material was tied in bunches, or seeds and other materials were sewn onto it, before it was plunged into a bath of dye. The protected spots came out white against the darker background. Resist dyeing also included *batik,* in which the design was painted with some kind of protective paste before dyeing.

Other imaginative and interesting fabrics were created in West Africa, such as the unique appliqué work, which used to be reserved exclusively for the king in Dahomey. Both the Yoruba and Bakuba wove fabrics with a plush effect, like velvet. And some tribes, like the Bamun, a Bantu tribe in the Cameroun highlands, decorated their cloth with embroidery.

The art of making typically African pottery may well have begun in ancient Meroë, where it was distinguished for its brilliance and originality. We have already noted that the truly individual ceramic ware of Meroë was usually a woman's craft and was molded by hand, without a potter's wheel. This was also true of pottery in West Africa, where it was made by a coiling technique similar to that used in basketry, or by simply scooping out a lump of clay. Only the Hausa and Bakongo used a pottery wheel.

In some communities, the wife of the smith was traditionally the local potter. Customarily, the pottery was dried in the shade for several days and then fired. This was accomplished, as a rule, by covering the pots with heaps of brush and wood, which were burned a short while. In the Congo the pots were placed in a shallow pit with an air passage at the sides before they were covered with the brush.

The pots were usually treated to prevent porosity, either by applying plant juices or palm oil after firing or by using a resinous gum while still hot. A black smoke glaze was sometimes obtained by smoking the pot and rubbing it to a high polish. Decoration took many forms. Patterns were worked into the surface by incising or impressing it with pointed sticks or rough materials, applying braids of clay, or modeling in relief. Black and red oxide, or indigo, were often painted on for color.

Modeling in clay, like the making of clay vessels, was usually done by the women, but they were seldom allowed to participate in the work on clay religious sculptures.

The earliest terra-cotta figures yet found in western Africa are those of the Nok culture. Many fragments of their life-sized clay statues have been uncovered by archaeologists. The heads are in the best state of preservation and are executed in a powerful abstract manner. Ife also produced some magnificent terra-cotta heads, though these are fully naturalistic rather than abstract. They were produced in a mold and fired in ashes heated to about 300°F.

Africans used clay in many imaginative ways, such as reliefs on walls of houses, roof-top ornaments, architecture, fetishes, pipes, and various small figures. Among the latter are the interesting little images dating from the ancient kingdom of Krinjabo, in the southwest Ivory Coast. It is thought that they were modeled to commemorate deceased members of the royal or privileged families. The Ibo also fashioned red clay figure groups, which were placed in the yam shrine to serve as guardian spirits. The Bakongo made figure-shaped pottery vessels, and both the Ashanti and the tribes of the Cameroun grasslands made intriguing clay pipes. The Ashanti pipes were decorated with illustrations from proverbs, while those of Cameroun had figures and faces that were carved out of the clay in high relief while it was still wet.

Figure sculpture and pottery-making also overlapped each other in the making of jugs bearing effigies. These were made in either wood or pottery by several peoples, including the Bakuba, Bakongo, and Mangbetu of the Congo. It is doubtful, however, if the Mangbetu art is at all relevant to America, since it was far out of the slaving range.

Because building stone is rare on the continent, there is nothing in West Africa to compare with the splendid stone structures found at Zimbabwe, or at Kilwa on the east coast. However, much of West African architecture shows an impressive use of local materials such as mud, wood, or natural fibers.

In areas of Islamic influence, sun-dried clay was handled with great distinction. Whole settlements of flat, boxlike houses called *zinder* were punctuated with palaces and mosques that had grace and dignity. In the latter, the supporting wooden beams were set off against the walls; this formed one of their characteristic and decorative features. Clever use of these projecting beams, proliferating towers, and other devices gave a relief effect that was enhanced by the bright sun of the open savanna. Sometimes these buildings were built of sun-dried bricks and sometimes of mere lumps of clay, smoothed over.

An example of *Asho òkè* cloth *(aṣo,* cloth; *òkè hill).* Traditionally woven with predyed threads in four-inch widths up to ten yards long, either in plain cotton or cotton with a silk overweave, as shown. (Collection Old Slave Mart Museum. Photo, author)

*Adire* cloth, dyed with indigo by the resist method (tie-dyed). Note how the areas protected by tieing have "resisted" the dye and left a white sunburst against the dark background. (Collection Old Slave Mart Museum. Photo, author)

Effigy pot, Mangbetu. Several African tribes made effigy pots, including some from which slaves were exported, though it is doubtful if the Mangbetu were among them. (Courtesy, The Museum of Primitive Art)

Wolof hat, Senegal. Basketry foundation covered with beautifully dyed, soft leather decorations. Though often spoken of as "Moroccan leather," such leatherwork has been made by West African craftsmen for hundreds of years. (Collection Old Slave Mart Museum. Photo, author)

Man selects his building materials from the environment, so in the forested regions of West Africa vegetable fibers were used. A framework of wooden stakes, poles, or canes was tied with thongs of twisted bark. The spaces between these were then filled in with plaited mats or thatched with papyrus, reeds, rush, grass, or palm branches to form a compact structure. Often, the outer walls were smeared with clay. Gaily colored wall paintings or clay relief enlivened many of these structures, while others were embellished with carved wooden supporting posts. Some of the latter, like the famous Yoruba caryatids, are handsomely executed. Wooden door frames, doors, and rafters also lent themselves to decorative and symbolic carving.

The beehive hut was generally used by nomadic peoples because it could be transported easily from place to place. Another type of dwelling with a cone-shaped roof and cylindrical base was encountered more often. However, in the areas that formed part of the early kingdoms, such as Benin and Dahomey, the gable-roofed dwelling was most common. The roof often protruded outward on one side and was supported by wooden posts to form a shady veranda. Many of the residences of the Guinea coast and Cameroun consist of four rectangular houses built around a courtyard much like the Roman *empluvium*. Dapper's description of just such buildings in seventeenth-century Benin has already been given.

In some instances, two or more of these styles were combined. On the Cameroun Plateau, for instance, there were erected imposing palaces that were built on a rectangular plan but had tall, cone-shaped cupolas of thatch. The supporting posts and door frames were decorated with colorful compositions.

Color was utilized in many ways. Although paints and dyes were seldom applied to figure sculpture, they were frequently used to brighten the walls of a house, to ornament masks and towering headdresses, to color leather and textiles, and to decorate pottery. Painting the face with color in rings, dabs, or streaks was often a substitute for wooden masks and may antedate their use.

Paint was not applied with a brush but with a feazed stick or a feather. Colors were obtained from mineral, animal, and vegetable sources, such as soot, coal, clays, lime and plant ash, *tukula* (camwood), indigo, and certain tree barks and leaves. They frequently had symbolic meanings. White, for instance, was a symbol of supernatural forces, danger, and death. Black often represented the earth. Red implied energy, vitality, and joy. It was associated with fire and therefore had magical properties and was used at festivals of rejoicing and at ceremonies of initiation.

Many Muslim tribes, because they were prohibited from making figure sculpture by their religion, developed other flourishing crafts—notably, the making of glass beads, work in hammered brass, painted house walls, weaving, and especially fine leatherwork. Mungo Park, in his travels along the Upper Niger River in 1797, praised the excellent and beautiful colored leatherwork of the Mandingos with whom he accompanied a slave coffle on a 500-mile trip to the coast. He stated that, after carefully tanning and dressing the leather until it was soft and pliable, they commonly dyed it with bright colors. It was made into sandals, quivers, and *saphies* (fetishes or good-luck pouches), as well as sheaths for swords or knives, belts, pockets, and a variety of ornaments.

In West Africa, all the arts were very much integrated with one another. Dance, music, drama, and applied arts might all be combined in a single ritual or ceremony. Similarly, carving, painting, metalwork, clay modeling, weaving, embroidery, leatherwork, or beadwork were often used in two or more combinations in a single article. It was not unusual for motifs applicable to one material to be used on another, as, for instance, when basket-plaiting designs were applied to wood or metal.

Even though some crafts were reserved to a favored few, artistic expression was a vital part of the lives of everyone. In making the humblest or most utilitarian of articles, such as a hoe, an ax, a woman's comb, or a cooking utensil, the greatest pride and enjoyment was obtained from shaping it with care and beautifying it with some kind of decoration.

It was from this background that the African was wrested and taken to a new land—a land with an entirely foreign culture, a foreign religion, foreign customs and laws. But the interwoven nature of African culture already owed some of its origins to constructive stimuli from non-African sources, and the Afro-American slave drew on this heritage to acculturate himself in America. With this inheritance from Africa, his skills, his approach to art and craft, and, above all, with his intelligent adaptability, he managed both to survive and to grow, in spite of the stultifying handicaps of slavery. Thus he was able to contribute his own particular gifts to this new land he was to call his own.

Combs from Liberia. Those on the right with burned-in designs have iron teeth. The large one (left) is a simple example of decorative combs that are worn in plaited hair. (Collection Old Slave Mart Museum. Photo, author)

Ceremonial Po spoon, or rice scoop, Liberia. Similar in shape to many Afro-American examples. The African scoop is handed down from generation to generation as an honorific emblem of the chief's mother or wife, who controls initiation into the female secret societies. (Collection Old Slave Mart Museum. Photo, author)

Beaded crown or hat that once belonged to Mwata Yawa Newezi III, chief of the Lunda tribe (and father-in-law of Moise Tshombe). In Africa, entire thrones or figures are sometimes fashioned in beadwork. (The head on which hat is displayed is by Dave Davidson, a young black artist.) (Collection Old Slave Mart Museum. Photo, author)

# 3 TRANSITION

African basketmaker and the author, Dakar, Senegal.
The coiled basket held in the author's hands is a
connecting link between Africa and America. Identical baskets were made by Afro-American slaves and
are still made by their descendants. See pages 58-59.
(Courtesy, Ebony Magazine. Photo, Moneta Sleet)

The transition from Africa to America must have been extremely difficult. The Africans were, literally, torn "between two cultures," and struggled to adjust themselves to a new way of life while at the same time trying to retain what little they could of their African heritage. This was made especially difficult because there was a need to adjust not only to the European culture in which they found themselves, but also to the Africans of other tribes with whom they were thrown.

It must be understood that slavery in itself was not new to the African. The custom of enslaving war captives, criminals, or debtors had long been practiced in Africa, as it had in other civilizations. Therefore, we must not believe that the mere thought of being *owned* by a fellow human being was as traumatic for the African as it would be to a twentieth-century American. Today, the entire concept of slavery is repugnant, and the equal rights of men a cornerstone of democracy. We should keep in mind, however, that although there were two kinds of slavery in Africa, neither of them was exactly comparable to the same institution in America. In Africa, there were "domestic slaves," who inherited their servitude, and there were "war captives" or kidnapped victims from neighboring tribes who did not. The former might be likened to serfs in European feudal society. They had certain rights and privileges not enjoyed by the war captive. The war captive was regarded either as ritual goods (for the sacrifices required on the death of royalty or to appease powerful ancestors) or as export goods (to be exchanged for European commodities). It was this latter custom that encouraged intertribal wars and brought many of the ensuing victims here by way of the Atlantic slave trade. Since war captives were not restricted to a warrior class, the Africans brought to this country must have represented a cross-section of the population of their own land. There were among them kings and priests, traders and slaveholders, court officials, domestic slaves who either fought beside their masters or in place of them, women and children, and above all, many of the skilled craftsmen discussed in the preceding chapters.

Probably the most traumatic and detrimental aspect of American slavery for the newly imported African, aside from loss of freedom, was the loss of his religion, with its concomitants, king and ancestors. The family, the clan, and, beyond that, the tribe, were always of great importance in knitting the African's society together and giving it stability. Kinship was one of the main principles of social organization in African societies. Continuity of family was made even more important by the tradition of ancestor worship. All this was tied in with the mystical concept of the semidivine kingship.

Occasionally an American slave was able to have a family life of sorts, depending on the local "black codes," or slave laws, and the benevolence of his owner. But almost never could he trace his ancestry, with the possible exception of the upper castes, such as house servants or craftsmen. Certainly it was impossible to keep up the genealogical chain all the way back to the mythological divinity from whom he had descended. Thus, what had been of prime importance in his African culture was absolutely obliterated here. This had a vital impact on the artistic life of the imported African, since he had no need (or opportunity) in this country for the elaborate rituals that had produced such beautiful art objects in his African homeland.

Retention of African cultural elements, or "Africanisms," varied greatly in this country, because of a number of different factors. In the urbanized North, slaves were imported in small numbers, usually from the West Indies rather than directly from Africa. Thus, they were already somewhat accustomed to a European way of life, or "seasoned," as it was called. Representing many different tribal groups, and working either alone or with one or two others, the African became more quickly "acculturated," or accustomed to American life, than did most slaves in the South, where there was more opportunity to continue African customs.

On the large southern plantations there were some factors that helped the slave to bridge the gap between the two cultures, European and African, in spite of their many differences. For one thing, although there were some cities of note in West Africa, most of the slaves came from an agricultural society rather than an urban one. The cultivation of such crops as cotton, rice, or indigo was familiar to them. The work in the fields, the opportunity to hunt and fish occasionally, to plant a small "patch" of one's own, to spend some spare time at handcrafts such as woodcarving, basketry, or net-making, was not dissimilar to life in an African village—at least on a superficial level.

The African had come from a society in which the individual identified his welfare with the welfare of the group. Stringent behavioral patterns were set by that society, and punishment of infractions was harsh and swift. The individual was expected to share with others and in turn expected others to share with him. Land was not owned by individuals, but by the community or family. Gold did not belong to the commonality, but to the king. Suffering, even death, were sometimes required of the individual for the benefit of king or community. But if the king's demands seemed at times cruel and arbitrary (like the master's in America) the African nevertheless had the assurance of his patriarchal guidance and protection. All these aspects were more or less true of the plantation community.

Like many African villages, the large plantation was a communal organization in which certain people were assigned duties for the entire group. The success or failure of the crop affected all, master and slave alike. In lean years the slave might be sold to help cover indebtedness; food, clothing, gifts, and other perquisites would probably be curtailed.

There were other factors, too, in addition to the "communalized" or "socialized" form of plantation life, that helped the slave to bridge the gap between two cultures. The frequent splitting of families caused the children to have more contact with mother than with father, and inheritance of servitude came through the matrilineal line. Beside this matriarchal aspect of the society, the allocating of responsibilities and duties to various age levels was not unlike what the Afro-American had been accustomed to. In fact, almost as important as kinship in Africa is organization by age; it plays a vital role in maintaining social order and cuts horizontally across vertical bands of kinship.

As in Africa, there was a strong caste system in America. The plantation slaves had their own social stratification. The house servants were the aristocrats who guarded their positions jealously and tried to see to it that their own children inherited the same caste. Next in this social structure were the skilled craftsmen, and at the bottom of the scale were the field hands.

Regarding the individual practice of African customs, the rural slave had more opportunity to continue them than did his city cousin, who worked in closer proximity to his white master. This was especially true on the large plantations, where most Negroes worked in a segregated world. In the fields, either alone where the "task" system was used, or under a Negro driver when the "gang" system was practiced, he could sing the same rhythmical songs and chants, or adaptations of them, that had accompanied work in Africa.

*The Old Plantation.* Painting of a slave wedding by an unknown artist, it shows several Africanisms. Aside from the probable similarities in the dance steps, the custom of using scarves and canes as an integral part of the dance is widespread in Africa. The stringed instrument has been identified by scholars as a *molo,* the drum as a *gudu-gugu,* and the material of the headties as Yoruba cloth. See pictures on opposite page.

(Courtesy, Abby Aldrich Rockefeller Folk Art Collection)

The "rites of passage" (ceremonies that marked birth, puberty, marriage, and death) were of great importance in Africa. In America, in spite of legal bans on slave marriages, many shareholders insisted on a religious ceremony and allowed the slaves to have a wedding celebration. They were also tolerant of burial practices. In Africa, with its emphasis on the role of ancestors in the lives of their descendants, the dead had been honored with elaborate rituals, and the funeral was the climax of life. This pattern continued in America. Both occasions, marriage and death, provided opportunities for African survivals.

Reproduced here is a famous picture of a slave wedding from the Abby Aldrich Rockefeller Folk Art Collection in Williamsburg, Virginia. It has been much studied by scholars, who have identified at least six recognizable "Africanisms," or African survivals, in it, with their forms little changed. On the other hand, the object used in a Congolese funerary custom disappeared even though the custom itself survived: the Bakuba priest leaves a small decorated box at the home of the deceased; friends and relatives place gifts for the family, or for the dead, in an opening on one side. Rural South Carolina Negroes, until recently at least, placed a saucer at hand during the vigil for the dead, so friends and relations could make contributions to help the family. (This custom was described in Dubose Heyward's book, "Porgy," after Crown killed Robbins.)

When the slaves were released for holiday celebrations at Christmas and Easter (a form of reward recognized by slaveholders as an important factor in keeping the slaves happy and encouraging them to work), there were songs and dances, games, and tales. Without a written language, the African had long relied on the bard, or storyteller, to preserve the history, traditions, and folktales of the tribe, and this he could still do in America in the privacy of these gatherings. No doubt other African cultural elements, such as their world view, or magical practices and religious ideas, could also be discussed and kept alive on these occasions, because there were no whites present.

Thus, in regard to attitudes, music, folktales, dancing, or burial customs, African culture could survive, though changed by European influences and affected by the differences between various tribal groups represented in any one gathering.

These differences were not so great as one might think. In regard to language, for instance, the Sudanic family spoken by all the tribes of Upper Guinea had more resemblances to the Bantu languages of the Congo and Angola than they did to English. Apparently the tribes from Upper Guinea, such as the Yoruba, Fon, Fanti, Ashanti, and Ibo, who came here in the greatest numbers during the eighteenth century, imposed their common cultural beliefs gradually on the others. There were not enough of the minority groups on any one plantation to continue their own customs or to preserve their own language or dialect, so those of the more numerous tribes were gradually adopted. In some areas, particularly the Sea Islands of South Carolina and Georgia, the Angola, or "Gullah," slaves joined the ones from Upper Guinea in large numbers. In these localities today we find cultural remnants from both groups.

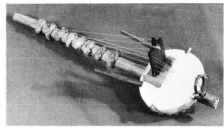

Kora. Stringed instruments such as this are common through Africa. It is similar to the *molo* shown in *The Old Plantation*, opposite. (Collection Old Slave Mart Museum. Photo, author.)

Yoruba *gudugudu* drum. Compare the drumstick, made of twisted leather, to that in the *The Old Plantation*, (Collection Old Slave Mart Museum. Photo, author)

Bakuba funerary box about 10 inches long. Made in the shape of a Bakuba coffin and embroidered with beads and cowries, it was used as a receptacle for gifts to the family of the deceased. Opening on side not shown. (Collection Old Slave Mart Museum. Photo, Jeanette L. Wragg)

*Laughing Nigerian Women*, by John Biggers. Note the similarity between the cloth of their headties and the bandannas in the painting opposite. (Photo, courtesy the artist)

Slave-made joggling board which was handed down in one family. Joggling boards were used like a trampoline by generations of white children throughout the South. This one is somewhat unique in that rockers have been added on each end. (Courtesy, Mrs. Samuel Lapham. Photo, author)

There is one African survival in the Sea Islands that is still very strong: the linguistic one. A few of the more obvious words, like goober, yam, canoe, and banjo, are well known. The distinguished Negro linguist, Dr. Lorenzo Turner, was quoted by Herskovits in 1940 as saying:

Up to the present time [1940] I have found in the vocabulary of the Negroes in coastal Carolina and Georgia approximately four thousand West African words, besides many survivals in syntax, inflections, sounds, and intonations. . . . I have recorded in Georgia a few songs the words of which are entirely African . . . African given names are numerous.

Herskovits goes on to explain that most experts in the Gullah dialect, such as Ambrose Gonzales of South Carolina, made a crucial mistake. Because of their lack of acquaintance with the vocabulary of certain African tongues, they interpreted as English what are in reality African words. He gives as one example the word *dzogal,* meaning in the Wolof language "to rise up," and interpreted by the Americans as a corruption of the English word joggle, or juggle. It was used to describe the popular joggling board, which at one time was found in every yard and playground in the South. It was a flexible, strong board, suspended between two stationary posts. Children amused themselves by bouncing up and down on it, trampoline-fashion. Truly it was a *dzogal* or rise-up board!

If indeed this word is of Wolof origin, it is exceptional, because the earliest arrivals, mainly Mandingos and Wolofs from the region between the Senegal and Gambia rivers, were, like the later ones from the African east coast, in the minority. They appear to have left little impression of their culture on America. Perhaps this is partly because the Mandingos were preferred as house servants and more quickly adopted European ways because of their proximity to white people. The whites early began to suppress many African customs, particularly those connected with religious or magical practices. All the customs surrounding the entrance into adulthood, for example, were strongly suppressed. These included the schools, of great importance in preserving African traditions, that had taught girls and boys tribal laws and prepared them for their place in society. This was partly because people tend to fear and mistrust things they do not understand, and white Americans found it impossible to understand the complex religions of West Africa. They also argued that one of the justifications for slavery was the opportunity to "civilize the savage"—by which they meant changing his culture from African to European. Thus, much of what the African retained had to be camouflaged or practiced clandestinely in order to avoid reprisals.

Still, many outlawed customs and beliefs continued to be quietly pursued in secret or carried on in disguised form. One cannot help wondering how many of the rituals and tabus that accompanied, say, the smith, in Africa, were continued in this country without the knowledge of white masters. Who knows what small ceremonies of preparation may have been carried on in private by carpenters or joiners before they cut into the "living" wood? Did they, too, like their African counterparts, pray to the tree for forgiveness? Did the black slave refuse to go behind a blacksmith while the iron was hot? Was it tabu to bring a rice fanner into the smithy for fear it would "spoil "its medicine? And were women forbidden to approach the forge?

Often, the white masters themselves absorbed more Africanisms than they themselves realized. A recent example of this came to light in Augusta, Georgia. There it was found, with the help of anthropologists and linguists on three continents, that several generations of white people had preserved, orally, a song in pure African tongue! Sung originally by an African princess who had become a slave nurse called Tina, it had been crooned to generation after generation of white babies, yet "Tina's Lullaby" had survived the years in perfectly intelligible, translatable form! It was the same language spoken today by the East African tribe from which Tina had come so many years before. Yet, to the white people who had preserved it, it was a meaningless rhyme!

Liberian carvings of the African Guinea hen. The origin of the word *Guinea* is uncertain, but it may be a corruption of *Ghana*. (Collection Old Slave Mart Museum. Photo, author)

Usually African customs practiced in secret by newcomers from Africa (called *bozal* or "salt water" slaves) were preserved in ever more garbled form by generation after generation of their descendants (the "country born"). As the original reasons for these customs faded, without the tribal schools to keep them alive, they often deteriorated into mere superstition. They were practiced from habit, or from some vague belief that they were connected with good or bad fortune.

One example of this is the Gullah Negro belief that to paint the doors and windows of a house blue "strains out the evil spirits." Though apparently superstition, it may have its origin in African religion. Blue has a special significance among Africans. Yemoja, among the Yoruba, is designated by the color blue as well as by patterns representing water and the universal ocean. Similarly, in many sections of the South it is considered bad luck to sweep a house after dark, possibly because of the African belief that the good spirits come to inhabit the house at night and can be swept out by mistake along with the dust. These are but a few of many examples, which sometimes can even be definitely traced to a particular tribal group. For instance, "voodoo" in Louisiana contains obvious elements of Dahomean religion because the French preferred slaves from Dahomey to all others.

Certain aspects of African religious cults were kept alive by Negro midwives, conjurers, and root doctors, and many of the customs and ideas associated with the planting of crops were carried over to this country. In Africa, for instance, the benne seed (African sesame) is used in fertility rituals. Brought to this country by slaves, and later as a "good-will" crop by the masters, it is still planted by rural Negroes in South Carolina. Sowed at the end of a field, it is said to bring good luck to the crop. The original ceremonies are gone, but the Gullah Negroes of the South Carolina and Georgia coast still connect this seed with the idea of fertility.

Other edible crops were brought over from Africa by the slave-owners to augment their own food, or to please the palates of the slaves, and these helped to bridge the gap between Africa and America. Cowpeas were one of these. They are still served in South Carolina in the traditional festival dish, called "Hoppin' John," at Christmas and New Year's. Others were watermelon and yams. (Though the word "goober" is of African origin, the peanut is not, since it was introduced to Africa from America.) Gourds, also native to Africa, were and still are put to many uses by rural Negroes in the South. They may be seen dangling from poles as birdhouses or used as dippers and bowls as in Africa, though they do not appear ever to have been decorated as they were in the mother country. The "guinea hen" was an African fowl introduced to this country. Until quite recently it was a familiar sight in every barnyard in the South. Okra, the African plant so popular in the southern United States in soups and gumbos, also dates back to slave days. The word *gumbo* is said to come from the African *kingombo*, which was what the Afro-American slaves called okra when it was first introduced into this country at New Orleans. *Okra* on the other hand, is the Akan name for the person who is the embodiment

Hand-carved wood shuttle, made by an Afro-American slave. Dr. Colin Turnbull, noted Africanist, believes it was carved with an adze, African fashion. (Collection Old Slave Mart Museum. Photo, author)

Fish net, for casting, made by the late Joe Deas, of John's Island, S.C., an expert craftsman who carved his own bone needles and made and used his nets much as his forefathers did in Africa. The slide is made of horn, a material frequently used in Africa. (Collection Old Slave Mart Museum. Photo, author)

Peter Alston, employee of The Old Slave Mart Museum, with rice ditch scoop from Laurel Hill Plantation, Va., and rake made of a sapling. (Collection Old Slave Mart Museum. Photo, author)

of the ruler's soul or spirit. How it came to be applied to the plant is uncertain.

(On a recent trip to West Africa, the author was entertained at the home of a Senegalese and served what was described as a "typical African meal." It could just as accurately have been called a "typical South Carolina meal," or "Soul Food," for the main dishes were "Charleston red rice," and fish gumbo, cooked with tomatoes, okra, and red peppers!)

Most Africanisms are difficult to assess without extensive specialized knowledge of African culture. Such things as "motor instincts," social or religious patterns, survival of pure African words and syntax in American Negro dialects, and similarities in dance and music all need their own specialists to detect.

In art and craft, too, it is necessary to have a knowledge of African counterparts to recognize their American descendants. There are few objects made by Afro-American slaves that can easily be seen by anyone as carryovers from African culture, because we are not apt to find any art form in this country identical to one in Africa. Most of the visual arts in America were intended for Caucasian use, and the slave-craftsman had to conform to European tastes and ideas. No American slaveholder wanted to have his mantel carved with stylized symbolic designs reflecting African concepts. He was homesick for reminders of his own mother country. Thus, the styles employed were generally reflections of European ones—mansard roofs, Adams porticoes, Palladian or Greek Revival facades, Wren church steeples, Chippendale or Hepplewhite furniture. Mantels and doorways were decorated with figures from Greek mythology, with egg and dart, Greek key, or other neoclassical motifs.

Therefore, in searching for survivals of African culture in slave-made objects, we must know where to look. They are unlikely to be found in any articles made primarily for use by Caucasian Americans, whether or not they were slaveholders. Some examples of Africanisms may be found, however, in those articles made for personal use by the slaves themselves. Often these were strictly utilitarian in character and merely followed the shapes, materials, and techniques of the mother country. But occasionally an object was decorated or embellished in some way that was reminiscent of Africa. Among the utilitarian items were agricultural and domestic tools and utensils—rice fanners, weaving shuttles, rice scoops, hoes, rakes, articles of clothing, etc. Decorative objects included small articles whittled for amusement or as gifts—for instance, pipes, canes, or musical instruments.

Dr. Lorenzo Turner has noted that the stringed instrument in the slave wedding picture mentioned earlier is a *molo*, found among the Hausa and Yoruba people of Nigeria, and that the drum is a Yoruba instrument called a *gudugudu*. The presence of the latter indicates that this picture must be a very early one, since drums very soon disappeared from the scene. Fear of slave revolts gave rise to slave codes forbidding their use. This was partly due to ignorance: the white people knew that Africans could send messages by drums in some way and assumed it was done by means of a code. Actually they are sent on a particular type of drum that can produce a variation of sounds similar to African vowels or words. These "talking drums" are shaped like an hourglass, with thongs stretching between two drumheads. By holding the drum under the arm and alternately applying and releasing pressure on the thongs, the tone of the drum can be changed, much as a kettledrum is tuned. Other kinds of drums cannot do this. Not knowing this, the whites forbade the use of all drums.

This very prohibition, however, gave rise to the one original American musical instrument, the banjo. Its ancestor was the "chordophone," a stringed instrument that is common throughout Africa. It evolved from a simple hunting bow, the single string being tapped by the arrow. Basically, the African instrument consists of strings that cross a drumlike resonator, like the American banjo. Adoption of it by the slaves gave them the percussion they lacked without drums. Together with hand-clapping and the rattling of "the bones" (which were literally dried animal bones), the banjo supplied the Negro with the beat for his songs and dances.

Slave-made tools or utensils are related to Africa in various small ways—the use of an adze rather than a knife for whittling or carving, the shape of a rice scoop, or perhaps the method of making a piece of pottery—and African ingenuity in utilizing natural materials at hand was applied by the slave on the American plantations. A fishnet was given a slide made of marrow bone or cow's horn. A chair seat was woven of twisted corn shucks; a tree branch ingeniously adapted into a rake or pitchfork. Such rakes were made from hickory saplings that had three or more branches to form the prongs. After the prongs were spread apart, they were held in place by a piece of wood with holes through which the prongs extended. The rake was then hung from a rafter with weights on the end so that it would dry with a straight handle.

Sometimes a familiar African form was transferred to another material, as in the case of a slave-made piece of pottery that resembles a carved wooden cup and was found in Bath, South Carolina. Or, again, a slave-made pipe was decorated with the same basketweave found on African pieces of wood or metal. This is in itself an Africanism. We have already seen that transference of patterns from one material to another was common in Africa.

Many iron tools and utensils have survived. Pottery is more rare, although Georgia and South Carolina both have excellent clay for that craft. Fine imported china and pottery were more common for use at the master's table, while metal or wooden vessels were used in kitchen and slave quarters. There is evidence, however, that some plantations did use local clay to make their own utensils and Negro slaves were employed in professional pottery kilns such as the one at Bath, South Carolina.

The pieces of clay-ware that have come to light thus far sometimes follow European traditions; one, in particular, is very like the English "Toby jug." But some do show African influence. By far the most interesting of these are the water jugs called "monkey pots" by the Negroes and "grotesque jugs" or "voodoo pots" by many museums, though it is very doubtful if these jugs were ever used in cult ceremonies. The name "voodoo" was applied somewhat indiscriminately by white people to anything that looked "heathenish" to them. On the other hand, the term "monkey pot" has an authentic origin. Mrs. Alice Davis, Negro artist on the faculty of Paine College, Augusta, Georgia, has explained this. According to her, the name was not a derogatory or descriptive one, as some have thought. It derived from the old-time expression, "I see a monkey," which was exclaimed by field hands when dizzied by the heat. The pots were used to prevent the "monkey" by bringing water to thirsty slaves working in the fields. There are definite resemblances between some of these jugs and African effigy pots.

Effigy jug, called a monkey pot by Negroes. It was made in Bath, S.C., about 1817 and is a dark bronzy brown with a beautiful high glaze. Its strong face has obvious African characteristics—the bold, stylized design and the exaggerated features. (Courtesy, The Augusta Museum. Photo, author)

It is not surprising that the monkey pot above resembles this Bapende wooden cup. In America men were the potters, though in Africa this was women's work. Therefore a man would be likely to use designs he was accustomed to making in wood. Such transference of patterns from one material to another is common in Africa. (Courtesy, University Museum)

Clay pipe, found by Peter Alston under a slave cabin in Awendaw, S.C., in 1968. The stem of the pipe is a single section of a hollow reed. Many such pipes have been found on the plantations of South Carolina. Note the raised design. (Collection Old Slave Mart Museum. Photo, author)

Coiled baskets made by Mrs. Ida Wilson and her family. (Collection Old Slave Mart Museum. Photo, author)

Pipe from Cameroun shows stippled design like that of the pipe from South Carolina. Abstract designs on African carvings appear to us as pure decoration, but to the African they are functional and symbolic. Such oblique Africanisms may lie unnoticed in many other slave-made objects. (Old Slave Mart Museum Picture Collection)

A contemporary flower basket by Mrs. Ida Wilson beside a slave-made rice fanner. These larger baskets have been strengthened with rush. The fanner is the connecting link between Mrs. Wilson's work and that of her African forebears. All three are made in identically the same way. (Collection Old Slave Mart Museum. Photo, author)

Liberian broom made of palm fiber. Similar to brooms made by Negroes in the southern United States, though the handles of the latter were longer. (Collection Old Slave Mart Museum. Photo, author)

Painting of a Charleston shrimp vendor by Edwin Harleston. Note the fly whisk, made of grasses. (Collection Old Slave Mart Museum. Photo, author)

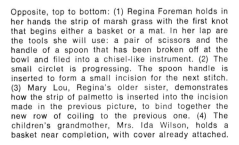

Opposite, top to bottom: (1) Regina Foreman holds in her hands the strip of marsh grass with the first knot that begins either a basket or a mat. In her lap are the tools she will use: a pair of scissors and the handle of a spoon that has been broken off at the bowl and filed into a chisel-like instrument. (2) The small circlet is progressing. The spoon handle is inserted to form a small incision for the next stitch. (3) Mary Lou, Regina's older sister, demonstrates how the strip of palmetto is inserted into the incision made in the previous picture, to bind together the new row of coiling to the previous one. (4) The children's grandmother, Mrs. Ida Wilson, holds a basket near completion, with cover already attached.

On the American plantations, basketry was preserved in purer form than most other crafts. Shapes, uses, and technique of manufacture are similar to those of Africa. Adults taught this art to children exactly as it had been taught to them, so that the method continued without interruption. Coil basketry has survived in South Carolina almost unchanged to the present day, so we can observe it firsthand. In the limited area where it is still practiced (along Route 17 north of Charleston, South Carolina), the craft is still perpetuated by the same apprentice system as in Africa. Boys, as well as girls, learn how to "sew" baskets. Once the boys reach puberty, however, they leave basket-making to the women until they attain old age, when they again take up the "sewing" as a pastime and to augment their meager incomes. The small children usually confine themselves to flat mats, beginning with small coasters and working up to the larger table mats of all sizes. Only the older experts weave the larger baskets, some of which are several feet high. The materials used for these baskets are identical to those used in Africa. Both are made of wild grass found on the edge of the marsh, and bound with strips of palm or its South Carolina relative, the palmetto. The only difference is that the South Carolina basketweavers have added the brown needles of the long-leaf pine for decoration. Larger baskets are strengthened in the center section with "rushel," a tough rush that is much thicker and stronger than the marshgrass customarily used for the core. Herskovits mentions in *Myth of the Negro Past* that the Sea Island basket-making techniques are also African in what he calls "motor habits," or the physical way of doing things. Both the African and the South Carolina baskets are laid on in a clockwise direction.

The American plantations needed the same kinds of containers that had been used in the agricultural societies of West Africa—vegetable, egg, or fruit baskets to carry on the head (both Africans and Afro-American slaves carried head-loads), baskets to hold cotton, and rice fanners. Brooms, fly whisks, and many types of mats were also made of vegetable fibers and remained virtually unchanged when adapted for use in this country.

Rice culture in the Low Country of Georgia and South Carolina was carried on in the African way, and it was still done in this fashion as recently as 1926. Rice was not considered good in antebellum days unless it was freshly hulled. On the plantations it was beaten fresh every day, and the pestles and mortars used became shiny like metal from constant friction. Two boys or two women did the pounding in one of two ways, depending upon the section where the rice was grown. One was to make an up and down motion, then rubbing back and forth, with each of the two people taking turns. The other was to pound up and down without rubbing. The beaters seized the pestles in the middle, raising them and letting them fall so quickly and evenly that the beating of the rice was not considered a difficult task, although often the pestle would be tied to the limb of a tree so the tension would pull the pestle up to aid in the task. Children who tried to pound the rice seldom succeeded, as it required a knack they did not possess. One of the "motor habits" mentioned by Herskovits is the tendency of Negroes to work as rhythmically as possible. The pounding of the pestles in the mortars of American plantations was as regular and rhythmical as the sound of the African drum.

After the rice was loosened from the husks, it was placed in the flat-bottomed baskets called "fanners," held high, and allowed to fall into baskets placed on the ground; the wind blew the chaff away. This process, which was called "fanning the rice," was repeated until the rice was perfectly clean. The rice-fanner was identical to those used in Africa for hundreds of years, as

Mrs. Wilson stands in front of her road side basket stand. She holds in her left hand the marsh grass which forms the core. A small bunch of palmetto fronds, torn into thin strips, is in her right hand. These materials are readily available along the South Carolina coast. (Photos, author)

Cane carved by Henry Cudgell, a slave from Ohio. It is intricately carved with a snake, turtle, and lizard or alligator. These are frequently encountered in African symbolism. Sometimes the snake is doubled and entwined like a medical caduceus, a design that has been recorded on slave-made conjurer's sticks. (National Gallery of Art, Index of American Design)

Charleston street vendor, about 1900. Note head-tie and African manner of balancing head-loads. (Johnson Photo Collection. Courtesy, Carolina Art Association, Gibbes Art Gallery, Charleston, S. C.)

Ashanti brass weight in the form of a man pounding grain with mortar and pestle similar to those used on the rice plantations of South Carolina. (Collection Old Slave Mart Museum. Photo, author)

The slave house of Mme. Metoyer, Natchitoches, La. Dr. Robert Thompson of Yale University feels it is reminiscent of the Bamalike houses of the Camerouns in West Africa. Note the wide, overhanging eaves. (Courtesy, Natchitoches Chamber of Commerce)

"The Street," slave quarters, Mulberry Plantation. A watercolor done about 1750, showing cabins with typical African style roofs. (Courtesy of the Carolina Art Association, Gibbes Art Gallery, Charleston, S.C.)

Children in South Carolina with rice mortar and pestle, about 1900. (Old Slave Mart Museum Picture Collection)

Slave-made rice mortar and pestle from a rice plantation, on the North Santee River in South Carolina. It is made of a hollowed out cypress log. (Collection Old Slave Mart Museum. Photo, M. B. Wilson)

were the rough-hewn pestle used for pounding and the mortar itself, a hollowed-out log.

Clothing, for the most part, conformed to European standards, though the indigo-dyed homespun cloth used for slaves often resembled West African "country cloth." A certain amount of latitude was allowed in the matter of headgear, and the women continued the African custom of wearing "headties" (or, as they were called in this country, "bandannas"). Headties have an important function in the life of African women because of the significance attached to their names and to various ways of tying them. Herskovits said he recorded over fifty different proverb names for styles of tying kerchiefs among the Ashanti alone. (In Haiti, a white handkerchief designated a *mambo,* a priestess of the *Vodun*—voodoo—cult.) Under the headties, slave women dressed their hair in African fashion. This was not at all like the "Afro" hair-style so popular today: it consisted of innumerable bits of hair that were tightly twisted or wrapped with cloth or string or made into myriad "plaits," or braids. These were arranged in various ways common in Africa. One such was the style called "corn rows," familiar to many of the older generation today and becoming popular among many younger black women.

Slave houses, too, were occasionally built in African style. Dr. Robert Thompson of Yale University has called attention to the resemblance of the Slave House of Madame Metoyer and the houses of the Bamelike, and Mr. Michael Cohn of the Brooklyn Children's Museum has noted the slaves' use of circular buildings and of rammed earth, which are also African architectural details.

From time to time, interesting discoveries have been made beneath these buildings. A metal figure was uncovered in an old slave smithy at Stony Point, New York. Dr. Colin Turnbull, the noted African ethnologist, says the figure is strongly African in spirit because of its stance—palms facing each other, legs and arms apart—as well as its small head. Perhaps it represents *Ogun* (Onsa), the Yoruba deity of iron, war, smithing, and hunting; or *Gu,* god of arms and war among the Fon of Dahomey.

Beautifully carved canes were made by Negroes for the use of the black conjurers, or "obeahs." Called "cunjer sticks" in South Carolina, they resemble the "juju," or magic sticks of Africa, and probably served some of the same purposes. They are among the few examples of original slave art done in African fashion, both as to the symbolic serpents and other totems or symbols, and as to the techniques of carving.

Two other interesting examples of Negro woodcarving are worth mentioning. One is a small seated figure made in Fayetteville, New York, around 1850. It is obviously similar to the shrine offering bowls of West Africa and the Congo, which are often in the form of a seated or kneeling figure holding a bowl. In this case, the "bowl" or container is held by a youth wearing European-style clothes. The other notable piece is the figure of George Washington carved at the top of a post, by a slave in Missouri. His lack of arms could be a result of African influences. White carvers probably would have shown at least vestigial arms, but this would be considered unimportant to an African. He stresses the parts of the body he feels are relevant to the particular piece he is working on—exaggerated sex organs in a fertility figure, for instance. In this case, the head, which denotes power and intelligence, was no doubt felt to be the most important feature to be stressed in representing the President of the United States.

Wood carving of a youth allegedly carved by a Negro employee for the daughter of Hiram Wood, owner of a grist mill in Fayetteville, N.Y., about 1850. Compare this with the Yoruba offering bowl above. Here, the "bowl" appears to be a wooden tub, and the figure is wearing European-style coat and pants. (Top, courtesy, Ladislas Segy. Bottom, courtesy of the Abby Aldrich Rockefeller Folk Art Collection)

Right, carving made by a slave in Missouri. The head has a strong resemblance to portraits of George Washington. Note that it has no arms. Above, armless *Akuaba*, or Ashanti fertility doll. Most of these dolls have vestigial arms, but armlessness per se is not in itself unusual in African figures. (Slave carving, National Gallery of Art, Index of American Design. *Akuaba*, Collection Old Slave Mart Museum. Photo, author)

Intriguing possibilities are presented by the discovery of a fleur-de-lis from a Gothic-style church that, on close examination, appears to represent a human figure. Is it possible that, hidden unnoticed within European art forms, slave-artists tried to express themselves in African fashion? If a slave-artist, presumed by his white masters to be making a French fleur-de-lis, can turn it into a human figure, what else may turn up that has been overlooked heretofore? Will we find a circle and dot mixed into the Adams motif on a plantation mantel? Do the intricacies of a wrought-iron gate hide an African basket-weave or zigzag design?

Whatever the answer, the slave did find various small ways to preserve remnants of his African past, and almost unknowingly, the Caucasian also absorbed and adopted many bits and pieces of African culture and incorporated them into what we call our "American Heritage." Music, dance, folktales, and cooking often show such obvious African influence that it has been generally recognized for years. There is no doubt, however, that Africa had a profound influence on the visual arts in America. It is not as obvious as in music or dance, and we must look more closely to discover it, but it is a search that is no less rewarding.

But because African motifs were superseded by European designs, the Afro-American slave's primary contribution to the visual arts in America came through his expert skills, and his familiarity with a variety of techniques. These skills, brought with him from his African homeland, were put to use from the very beginning.

Fleur-de-lis that resembles a small human figure. From a Gothic-style Huguenot church, Charleston, S. C. (Collection Old Slave Mart Museum. Photo, author)

Child's suit of blue and white country cloth from Liberia. This suit was brought to the United States by an ex-slave seaman named Clement I'On, who captained one of the first ships to ply between the United States and Liberia. The suit was a gift to the people who had manumitted him. The material, dyed with indigo, is similar to much of the "slave cloth" worn by American Negro slaves. (Collection Old Slave Mart Museum. Photo, author)

# 4 URBAN CRAFTSMEN

Courthouse, Vicksburg, Miss., built entirely by slaves.
From an early engraving showing General Grant's
entry into the city. (Courtesy, Old Courthouse Museum,
Eva Davis Memorial, Vicksburg, Miss.)

Life in the American colonies in the early days was full of hardships and difficulties. There was much to be done, with too few hands to do it. Enslavement of the Indians (against the expressed terms of treaties and laws) engendered bloodthirsty reprisals and massacres. Indentured servants brought from Europe could easily escape detection when they ran away because they could blend into the white community. Therefore they were a liability to the man who had paid for their indenture. And so the African, largely because of his color, gradually replaced the Indians and whites of the early days and became the answer to the colonies' labor shortages.

It did not take the white masters long to discover that many of these Africans were skilled craftsmen who could be used more profitably turning out material goods than laboring in field and forest. Everything was needed at once in the new land, and the only way to obtain it was literally by manufacturing, or hand-making, it. So the need for craftsmen, or "mechanicks" as they were called, was great. This situation changed little from the colonial period to about 1830, when the Industrial Revolution began to alter the structure of the nation.

On the whole, the South was at first not quite so dependent on locally made articles as was the more urban North. In days of barter and exchange the agrarian southern colonies were less hampered by restrictive British laws concerning what they could or could not export. They exchanged tobacco, pine tar, and turpentine—and, later, rice, indigo, and cotton—to earn profits in the form of credit in England for buying many of their needs. So the Southerners made fewer things for themselves, at least in the port cities where imports were available.

Nevertheless, prices for the imported articles were high—about three times the normal English prices—and ships were few and far between. So there arose an increasing demand for more and more locally made articles. Anger over heavy British taxation made it a matter of conscience to patronize local craftsmen. Political and religious upheavals in Europe, counterbalanced by the growing stability of the colonies, hastened the immigration of skilled artisans who then began to train American apprentices (both black and white) in their "trades." The revocation of the Edict of Nantes in 1685, for instance, which drove hordes of French Protestant craftsmen to South Carolina, helped to develop Charleston as a center for American-made handcrafts. These newly arrived craftsmen were concentrated in the cities, where the demand was greatest. Although most of them accepted a variety of work, as competition and population increased so did specialization. The pioneer situation that required everyone but the wealthiest slaveholder to satisfy all his own needs slowly gave way to centralized communities where articles could be purchased from specialists. In order to accommodate the increased trade, the majority of the independent artisans employed help in the form of apprentices, either indentured servants or slaves.

The number of Negroes available for this type of work varied during the colonial period according to location, from New Netherlands (New York), where Negroes were always highly valued but few in number, to Georgia, where they were entirely banned until 1750. Later, slaves were more numerous all along the eastern seaboard and the Gulf of Mexico. In the Carolinas, slavery was not only sanctioned by the Constitution, but slaveholders were also encouraged by the gift of extra acreage for every Negro slave brought into the colony. Charleston, the major seaport of the Carolinas, therefore became a great center of Negro craftsmen, as did New Orleans.

The records in South Carolina show that the majority of the white artisans owned black slaves and greatly valued their skills as assistant craftsmen. Some of these Negro apprentices were purchased at random from incoming shiploads of Africans. In general, however, artisans preferred to purchase or hire them from some large slaveholder who had discovered skills or aptitudes in advance. An astute owner was unlikely to put a Negro to the plow if it were learned through an interpreter that he already had extensive experience as a smith. The returns on a trained craftsman were too high to waste such a man in the fields.

Urban craftsmen produced a variety of stock articles, which were sold in shops, as well as "bespoke work," objects that were custom-made to the buyer's own particular specifications. Among these craftsmen were the *Peruke-maker* (wigmaker), the *weaver* and the *fuller*, who used complicated techniques for preparing homespun woolen cloth for use, the *chandler*, who is known today as a ship supplier but who at that time had to make the beeswax or whale-oil candles, tallow dips, and rushlights that preceded electricity. He also made soap. The *hatter* had an important and exacting business: in those days a man would as soon have gone without his head as without a hat. The demand for his goods was always high, and it required laborious and exacting work to turn fur into felt and then into hats. The *housewright* employed men of many skills. There were *carpenters* and *joiners*, the latter being those who did the more skillful work, such as paneling, moldings and cornices, stairways or mantels. To them also fell the job of making window frames and sashes. Occasionally, if he were very skillful, a joiner might even turn his hand to making furniture, though this was normally the specialty of a *cabinet-maker*. The housewright also employed *sawyers*, who were, in the days before the circular saw was invented (ca. 1814), the men who changed rough logs and timbers into planks; at times they were called upon to prepare the delicate shingles for the roof. *Brickmakers* and *masons* might also be in the housewright's service.

*Ironmasters, papermakers,* and *glassblowers* worked in factories in teams. So did braziers, who produced such cast-brass and bronze objects as bells or brass buttons. *Glaziers* usually doubled as *gilders* and made mirrors or gilded their frames as well as set panes of glass in windows. They also laid the gold leaf so popular as trim on coaches or signs. In the days when many people were illiterate, the shop sign had to be easily identifiable. It served as an address, too, before the days of street numbers. So the *sign-maker* was a necessity. Many of the signs pictured the object for sale, either on a flat board or as a three-dimensional object in wood or metal.

The *hornsmith's* work was particularly important before the invention of plastic or cheap glass. By soaking, splitting, and cutting, he could turn animal horn into many useful objects. He made translucent panes for lanterns, combs, and horn or tortoise-shell frames for eyeglasses. Other smiths included the *locksmith* and *gunsmith*, the *blacksmith*, the *whitesmith* or *tinsmith*, the *coppersmith*, and the *silversmith*. Although the latter sometimes called himself a *goldsmith*, this may have been a pretension. American silversmiths made little gold jewelry and much that they sold was imported. The *pewterer* and the *plumber*—any craftsman who worked in lead—might also be included with the smiths.

The *wainwrights*, who made sedan chairs as well as coaches and chaises, also employed a wide range of workers: *wheelwrights, blacksmiths, wood-workers, trimmers,* and *upholsterers*, as well as *painters* and *gilders*. They might even have a *leatherworker* as well, for coach bodies rode on leather

Slave-made shingle and *froe*, a splitting tool with a thick wedge-shaped blade that was driven downward along the wood grain to make the shingles. About 1856. (Collection Old Slave Mart Museum. Photo, author)

slings called thoroughbraces, and even after springs were commonly used the carriage bodies hung from them on leather straps.

A few of the trades were established outside of towns. Unless employed by artisans who did "bespoke" work, the sawyers generally worked at a permanent sawpit on the outskirts of the community. The brickyard that made bricks or tiles was probably nearby. The *shipwright* worked near a place where he could launch his boat, and the *miller* was usually in a rural area. Foundries were often located on or near wharves, probably as a convenience to water for transport or to reduce the fire hazard.

The *tanners* were early banned from the cities because of the stench they created, but *saddlers* and *shoemakers* had their shops in town. Leather was used for shoes, belts, saddles, and bags, but it had many other uses: high boots were a necessity in the muddy unpaved streets and roads; artisans wore tough leather aprons; and many men wore leather breeches.

*Bookbinders, lensgrinders,* and *cabinetmakers* usually had their shops in the city. So did the *coopers* and the *white coopers;* the former constructed the heavy barrels and hogsheads used for shipping and storing the local produce. The latter made the small measures, sieves, and boxes out of thin strips of wood, as well as military drums. Both crafts called for a high degree of skill and were much in demand.

The ladies were *dressmakers* and *seamstresses,* both employed in the home, and *mantuamakers.* The latter were more fashionable dressmakers who had shops where they displayed the latest styles from London and Paris on tiny "fashion-plate dolls."

Newspapers from the colonial period show that white mechanics invested consistently in slaves, and many of them left wills specifically mentioning ownership of black artisans. Having trained and sold Negro craftsmen to townsmen and planters, the white artisans of South Carolina were greatly annoyed when the purchasers hired out those same slaves in competition with the sellers. This brought about unemployment, and the system was most loudly denounced. Letters, bills of sale, handbills advertising sales of slaves, as well as advertisements for runaways, give further evidence that artisans often bought a slave, trained him (thereby enhancing his value), and then sold him. Sometimes they kept the enslaved craftsman to ensure the support of their families after death. In some cases, the trained slave was hired out to supply a widow with a steady income; if she were enterprising, however, she continued to carry on her husband's business with the aid of his slaves. Ann Hawes, the wife of a Charleston painter and gilder, continued her husband's trade with the aid of his employees after his death. Jane Inch, in Maryland, did the same. When her husband died, she advertised that "the silversmith's business, Tavern Keeping, and Boats to go up and down the Bay, are carried on as usual by Jane Inch."

For sale notices and advertisements for runaway slaves culled at random from the South Carolina *Gazette* of 1732 give just a scant idea of the variety of trades practiced by Negro craftsmen at that time; they mention sawyers, caulkers, carpenters, a bricklayer, a plasterer, a cooper, a ship's carpenter, and a shoemaker.

Nor were these all. In Charleston, South Carolina, Samuel Cardy, an architect, offered for sale a few "valuable slaves," "House Carpenters" among them. Ezra Waite of Charleston left among his effects when he died, "2 Negro fellows . . . one of them a bricklayer." Brickmakers John Fitch and Thomas Rose of Charleston, both owned Negro assistants; the former had one and the latter was the master of nine. In 1747, John Paul Grimke, a jeweler, offered to sell "about 13 or 14 Negroes," among whom was a "very good Cooper."

The same was more or less true throughout the South. In Mississippi, the Weldon brothers, Irishmen from Antrim, were housewrights who are known to have employed black craftsmen. They had one hundred skilled slave artisans who worked for them on a number of famous buildings in Mississippi, including the beautiful courthouse at Vicksburg.

At present we must rely mostly on scattered advertisements and references, and on wills, letters, and other family papers, for documentation about Negro craftsmen. Therefore it is impossible to state positively whether or not Negroes practiced in *all* the trades we have mentioned. Each year, however, more and more information on the work of eighteenth- and nineteenth-century Negro craftsmen comes to light. In fact, there is overwhelming evidence that Negroes made up a large proportion of the "base mechanicks" from colonial days to the present, and that they also made valuable contributions to our preindustrial society in trades that required a high degree of skill and artistic ability, such as wrought-ironworkers, cabinetmakers, pewterers, stucco workers, and silversmiths.

Silversmithing was a particularly responsible trade, and one practiced by many slaves. Since no assay office existed in America until 1814, it was left to the silversmith to keep his own silver up to the sterling standard. Yet no piece of colonial silver has ever tested below standard. Since the customer had to trust the smith, it was necessary that the latter have a reputation for integrity as well as skill. There are many records like the following:

George Dorwig—On Friday, the 13th of July, will be sold by Public Vendue . . . all the Jewellery and Silver Ware belonging to George Dorwig, Jeweller and Goldsmith; . . . likewise . . . a Negroe man, by trade a silversmith . . . *Penna. Gazette,* July 5, 1770

In the North as well as in the South the silversmiths had sidelines that included various other fields of art. Besides making most of the articles normally found at a jeweler's, they practiced all forms of engraving. Paul Revere, for instance, was not only a superb artist in silver, but he also engraved political broadsides, like his famous picture of Crispus Attucks and the Boston Massacre. Nor was Revere the exception. Other silversmiths made maps and engraved plates for printing paper money, trade cards, bookplates, and book illustrations, as well as sheet music. The cards and bookplates were not mere lettering; they were usually decorated with Grecian goddesses, or some kind of image of the business, and were surrounded by fancy borders.

There was a certain amount of overlapping in most trades, and many craftsmen commanded a number of different skills. One Negro man and his two sons, Caesar and Pompey, worked in the printing establishment of Thomas Fleet. All of them set type and did woodblock engraving as well. The father, whose name is unknown, was said to have "cut," on wooden blocks, all the pictures that decorated the ballads and small books of his master. This was not at all an unusual part of the printer's duties, and there were many other Negroes who worked at the printer's trade. Peter Timothy, editor and publisher of the South Carolina *Gazette,* was much beset by difficulties caused by white apprentices and journeymen printers, whom he had to fire because of their "unhappy affection for Drink, Play and Scandalous Company." He was finally left with no other assistance in his shop "excepting a Negro boy, whom I'm teaching to serve me at the Press."

Cigar-store Indian, said to have been carved by a slave named Job, in Freehold, N.J. (Courtesy, New York Historical Society)

Woodcarvers, too, worked at other trades besides printing and engraving. Both wallpaper and cloth had to be hand-stamped by a laborious process that called first for carving the pattern on a small block of wood. With "pitch pins" placed in each corner, the design could be repeated with exact registration. This process was similar to the direct" method of stamping used in Africa for *adinkra* cloth and other fabrics. Signs were often made in the round, like the cigar-store Indian said to have been carved by a slave named Job in Freehold, New Jersey. Shipwrights probably made their own figureheads, which were meticulously carved and painted. And when cast iron began to replace the earlier wrought-ironwork, the elaborate patterns of grapes or other fruits and flowers had to be carved first before the mold could be made.

There are many records of black ironworkers. Dr. James Porter mentions Isaac Weld, a British traveler who observed that in 1796 all the iron furnaces and forges in Maryland were worked by blacks; Porter also says that "by the last quarter of the Eighteenth Century Negro slaves and freemen partly or completely manned the iron manufacturing plants in the Southern Colonies." Charleston and New Orleans were particularly famous centers for wrought-ironwork and much of it was done by black craftsmen. In New Orleans, slaves of the pirate, Jean Lafitte, produced many of the beautiful examples there. In Charleston, Peter Simmons, a slave blacksmith, was well known. He taught his art to the contemporary black craftsman Phillip Simmons (no relation) who is still practicing in that city.

Much of the earliest ironwork in this country has been lost by fire and war. Some was melted down for military purposes during the American Revolution. Tradition has it that large amounts were used to shoe the draught and riding animals of the Continental forces. Some of the finest gates that escaped the Revolution were donated in Civil War days to the Confederacy to be used for the ironclads. Squads of men were detailed to pick them up in Charleston, South Carolina, and heavy wooden ones were substituted. Luckily, many stair railings and balustrades were spared, and a number of handsome examples remain.

The earliest inspiration for wrought-ironwork was of European origin. Some ironwork was actually imported and either wholly or partially imitated or incorporated into other pieces. But as American ironworkers increased, more and more work was done locally. The blacksmith sometimes used European pattern books, but some smiths, both black and white, created their own patterns. Whoever originated the design, the responsibility for its execution rested in the talented hands of the blacksmith. And in wrought-ironworking, more than most crafts, the act of translating a design from one medium to another provided exceptional opportunities for originality and artistry. The beauty of wrought-ironwork is largely a result of the fact that each curve or bar is hammered out step by step. The hot metal is placed between top and bottom tools known as "swages" and shaped with blows of a heavy sledgehammer. It is this act of shaping the softened metal that gives so much importance to the smith even when he is executing a design originated by another man. For when a pen or pencil drawing was interpreted in solid iron, the exactness of a curve, the diameter of a bar, and the finished size of the member or spaces between could determine whether or not a particular piece achieved the level of art. A good design could be ruined, but, conversely, a poor design could be improved.

In 1812, cast-ironwork was introduced into this country by Germans and began to replace the more delicate handforged work. This contributed to the decline of the latter, and after 1826 wrought-ironwork began to deteriorate

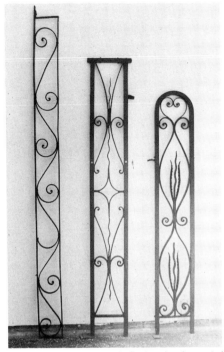

Slave-made wrought ironwork. Designed and executed by Peter Simmons of Mt. Pleasant, S.C. (Old Slave Mart Museum)

Gate, Murray Boulevard. Slave-made wrought ironwork. (Photo, author)

Plaster cast taken from an iron balcony in Natchez, Miss. Carving the pattern for this would challenge the talents of any woodcarver. (Collection Old Slave Mart Museum. Photo, author)

and the workmanship became mechanical. To a great extent, the creative act of hammering out the hot metal gave way to the use of standard-shaped pieces that could be fitted together, and the work lost its interesting handwrought look.

As we admire the ironwork in the cities and on plantations of the South, we can easily distinguish wrought-ironwork from its later rival. Cast iron is bulkier and less lacy than the former, though it is often very beautiful in its own right. Although cast-ironwork was heavier and more massive, it had a three-dimensional effect, which helped make up for its lack of the spiderweb tracery that characterizes wrought-ironwork. Grapes and other fruits were among the most popular motifs, and with the Civil War came guns and military emblems.

Cast iron is literally molten metal cast in molds. The pouring of the metal was more nearly a craft than an art. In this it was unlike wrought-ironwork, whose execution required artistic talent, as well as skill. It was in the creation of the pattern from which the mold was made for casting that artistry came into play. Such patterns, made of wood, were often exquisitely carved, and even utilitarian objects, such as gears for machinery, had to be formed of tiny, handmade pieces, first shaped with an adze or a knife and then glued together. These patterns were set into wet sand to form a mold into which the molten iron could be poured. They were coated with graphite to facilitate their removal from the sand; this gave them a glossy black color. Both decorative and useful objects were made out of cast iron. Stair rails, spindles, pilasters, elaborate iron balcony decorations, and cemetery memorials provided opportunity for artistic work, but more mundane objects such as gears and machinery for rice or sugar cane mills were also produced in large quantities.

The design for cast-ironwork might originate from a pattern book, though sometimes a drawing was made by the foundry master or by the architect who planned to use it. But the wooden pattern itself was most often made by a foundry worker, and in the South at least he was apt to be a Negro. The Riley Foundry, in Charleston, employed an ex-slave as chief patternmaker for many years, and he may also have worked for them as a slave before emancipation. It was common for Negro craftsmen in the South to continue working as employees of their former masters after emancipation. For this reason the black craftsman was in a better economic position than unskilled Negroes.

Craftsmanship offered the Negro slave both a means of earning his freedom and a way of supporting himself afterward. Although in the nineteenth century various states enacted laws aimed at reducing the number of free Negroes to a minimum, manumission never stopped altogether. Some slaves gained freedom through the termination of their indentures, or as a reward for an act of bravery; others were manumitted by a white father or by the will of their deceased master. A few were freed during the lifetime of a benevolent owner. But by far the largest number had to pay for their freedom in hard cash. The usual way for a slave to earn this was to persuade his owner to allow him to "hire his own time." Whatever was earned over and above the payment required by the owner could be credited to purchasing freedom. Since the craftsman was in particular demand as a hireling, he held an advantageous position. Craftsmanship could lead to self-hire, and self-hire was often a steppingstone to self-purchase.

Sometimes self-hire also aided a slave in making a dash for freedom. Robert Smalls, a slave owned by Henry McKee of Beaufort, South Carolina, first hired his own time as a sailmaker and rigger in Charleston, South Caro-

72

lina, and saved slowly toward his own and his family's purchase price. But his trade led to a quicker way. Having learned a harbor pilot's skills at his waterfront job, he seized *The Planter,* a Confederate steamer, and, with his family safely on board, stole out of Charleston Harbor under the very noses of the Rebels. Free at last, he turned the boat over to the Union Navy. A slave in Macon, Georgia, also used his earnings as a craftsman to aid in his escape. With money that cabinetmaker William Craft saved by hiring himself out, he purchased male attire for his light-skinned wife, Ellen. This enabled her to pose as a white planter and William as her black bodyservant. In this disguise they traveled northward toward freedom in first-class style.

The world of the free Negro was a difficult one. There was no room in it for anyone of a dependent nature. Therefore, a slave-owner was more apt to give encouragement to one who had the obvious means of self-support. This applied particularly to the skilled craftsmen, who were always in demand. Denmark Vesey, who led the 1822 slave rebellion in Charleston, was a case in point. He purchased his freedom with $600 won in the East Bay Street lottery. As a free man, he was able to support himself for twenty-two years as a carpenter in Charleston before he organized the revolt that led to his execution.

The free Negro had existed even before statutory recognition of slavery was enacted in this country. In 1790, free Negroes made up 7.9 per cent of the total black population. It rose to 13.7 per cent in 1830 and dropped in 1860 to 11 per cent. Many of these free men were property-owners; some were even slave-owners. To support themselves they held various business licenses and advertised their work in newspapers. They were listed in city directories and tax records as Free Men (or Women) of Color, or by the abbreviations FMC or FWC. Because of this, they are much easier to trace than their slave brothers. The records show that free Negroes tended to be urban, probably because of the greater economic and social opportunities in the cities. Dr. John Hope Franklin says that "by 1860 they were concentrated in six areas: the tidewater counties of Virginia and Maryland; the piedmont region of Virginia and North Carolina; the southern cities of Baltimore, Washington, Charleston, Mobile, and New Orleans; the northern cities of Boston, New York, Cincinnati and Philadelphia; isolated areas of the old Northwest . . . ; and communities where Negroes had mixed freely with Indians. . . ." Wherever they were, there was a wide variety of vocations among them, and craftsmen were high on the list. Dr. Franklin notes that there were more than 70 occupations in North Carolina, 100 in Boston, and 159 in Philadelphia, all of which involved the exercise of skills. Some free black men did engraving and photography; others were jewelers, architects, and lithographers. Almost every community had free Negro carpenters, cabinetmakers, brickmasons, and blacksmiths who did fine wrought-iron ornamental pieces.

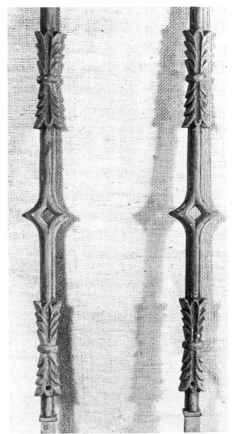

Cast iron stair rail spindles; made for the Dock Street Theater. (Collection Old Slave Mart. Photo, author)

Patterns for gears and machinery from the Riley Foundry, Charleston, S.C. (Collection Old Slave Mart Museum. Photo, author)

The following partial list from the Census of Free Colored People in the Charleston, South Carolina, Directory of 1856 gives us a glimpse of the variety of trades practiced by them:

| | | |
|---|---|---|
| 50 tailors | 6 blacksmiths | 1 molder |
| 6 wheelwrights | 2 cabinetmakers | 1 tinsmith |
| 65 carpenters | 4 dressmakers or | 1 sawyer |
| 9 mantuamakers |   seamstresses | 1 ship's carpenter |
| 2 coopers | 9 millwrights | 3 mattressmakers |
| 9 bricklayers | 6 painters | 1 jeweler |
| 11 shoemakers | 1 pumpmaker | 1 silversmith |
| 1 wharfbuilder | 2 shipwrights | 1 grist-miller |
| 1 dancing master | 2 locksmiths | 2 cotton-menders |
| 1 saddler | 4 bootmakers | 1 carpenter and coffinmaker |
| 1 finisher | 1 musician | |
| | (leader of the Cadet Band) | |

Some free craftsmen carried on their employer's trade after his death or when their former employer went into another line of business. In 1770, according to the *Gazette* of the State of South Carolina, a cabinetmaker named John Packrow had an enterprising Negro servant who left him and took over his master's former trade when Mr. Packrow went into the ferrying business. Offspring of free Negroes learned their father's trade as apprentices, and such skills were often handed down in the same family through many generations.

Negro craftsmen were more likely to employ other Negroes, either slave or free, as assistants and often purchased relatives who helped in their trades. But this was not always true. Thomas Day, a Negro cabinetmaker of Milton, North Carolina, employed a white journeyman for years. Day is one of the best known of the antebellum craftsmen. From 1820 to 1870, his furniture, which was "bespoke" by the richest clientele, was much sought after, even outside his own state.

In fact, whether they were slaves or whether they were free, Negroes distinguished themselves in many highly skilled crafts and trades. And there was no dearth of vocations that could put to good use the artistic temperament and the infinite capacity for taking pains that we call "craftsmanship." As boatload after boatload of Africans arrived in this country, memories of old-country techniques were constantly being refreshed by new arrivals from the Guinea coast. Thus, African skills and methods were preserved in this country even when other cultural elements were obliterated. And because art as craft so permeates African life and culture, aptitudes even survived for several generations in this country.

This survival was aided by the manner in which Africans were trained in America. The early arrivals, most of whom reached the shores of North America from the West Indies, were augmented by increasingly more frequent shiploads direct from Africa. In the early eighteenth century, newspaper notices abounded with references to arrivals from the Gold Coast (Ghana), from Calabar (Nigeria), and from Angola. Even that early, however, there were many "country-born" Negroes to train the newcomers. For instance, in February, 1732, in Charleston, South Carolina, there was "exposed to sail [sic] to the highest Bidder, the personal estate of Mr. John Godfrey, deceased, 42 choice Negroes, Men, Women and Children, Some of them Tradesmen [i.e., craftsmen] and the greatest part of them born in Carolina."

On arrival in this country from Africa, the "salt man" or "Bozal Negro," as he was called, was first apprenticed to an earlier arrival who was already seasoned but who still recalled enough of his African language to understand the newcomer. He served as interpreter and helped to accustom the African to the strange way of life in America. By careful selection, the Bozal Negro could be assigned work with which he was already familiar; under the tutelage of the "country-born," he could apply his African skills to needs in this country.

We have already seen that these needs gave the black craftsman few opportunities to create objects that were identical to those in his own culture. Those who worked on articles for the white master's use had to adapt their skills to turn out work in European style. The method and the materials, however, were the same. The blacksmith might have been trained in making spears, iron money, or anklets, but the techniques were the same for making mule-bits, tinsnips, or wrought-iron gates. The basket-maker, the weaver, the potter, the leatherworker probably had to make little adjustment between their former work and the new. The expert in bronze or brass could no longer make objects to glorify his king, but he had the basic skills needed for the transition to the job of brazier or silversmith. Perhaps the woodcarver had the greatest readjustment to make, since his work in Africa had been devoted largely to religious and cult objects. But results show that he, too, made the change, and adapted his skills to cabinetmaking, joinery, figurehead- or sign-carving, and many other crafts. And by preserving his techniques and pride of craftsmanship, the Afro-American was laying the groundwork for future contributions to American art and crafts that would be more personally rewarding.

# 5 PLANTATION CRAFTSMEN

Slave-made desk and chair from The Elms Plantation
near Millbrook, Ala. (Courtesy, Mrs. Alma Hall Pate.
Photo, Scott)

Though by far most of the skilled craftsmen, both slave and free, were to be found in the cities, information about them is sketchy. Much of it is statistical, obtained from city directories, advertisements, or tax records. From these we can learn how many Negroes were employed in a given trade and gain some idea of the wide variety of their vocations, and the value placed on their services. Both white and Negro craftsmen, however, worked anonymously for the most part, and public records give us only the barest information about specific artisans and their work.

This is not true of the slave on the plantation. Most of the largest slave-holders left journals, diaries, or private letters describing life on their estates and these give us a firsthand report. The works of slave craftsmen, both men and women, still exist, treasured as heirlooms by many a slaveholder's descendants. Many of the craftsmen are remembered by name or were known personally by the present owners of their work. Often the particular circumstances surrounding the creation of a piece of furniture or other object will have been preserved and oft repeated as a bit of oral family history. Thus, for descriptive information about slave craftsmen, their techniques and their productions, we need to examine some of these plantation records. Without them we would have no firsthand knowledge of the tremendous contributions made by these slave craftsmen.

Contrary to popular ideas, large slaveholdings made up only a small proportion of the whole. In 1860, less than 12 per cent of all slave-owners had more than twenty slaves. Many of them had fewer than five slaves. On these smaller farms we find few slave craftsmen and fewer records.

The owners, being poor, had to do a great deal of the work themselves and had little time or need for keeping records. The wife of the owner frequently did all the household chores, such as cooking and washing, as well as such crafts as weaving and spinning. A slave woman might help occasionally with these tasks, but she was probably expected to work in the fields as well. The master often worked with his field hands and might attend to most of the skilled craftwork himself, rather than purchasing an artisan, who brought some of the highest prices on the slave market. Or else he temporarily hired a slave craftsman from one of his more affluent neighbors.

The larger slave-owners ran their plantations like efficient factories; they were well organized and had to keep records and communicate with their overseers and stewards. Their holdings ranged from thirty slaves to the fabulous empire of that most efficient of all rice planters, Nathaniel Heyward, who, at his death, owned 2,087 slaves on several plantations. (This was an unusually large number, even for the wealthiest slaveholders, though many of them did own from 100 to 150.) The large plantations were like small villages and were almost entirely self-sufficient. Roads were poor, and journeys to the nearest city for purchases were made only on very rare occasions. In the tidewater sections of the eastern seaboard, rivers and estuaries were, of course, used for transportation, and in the marshy low country of South Carolina, master, family, and house-servants usually made a yearly trek to the city and remained there during the malaria season. Nevertheless, for most it was easier and more economical to supply their own needs.

At Belmead, a plantation on the James River in Virginia, the work journal shows that at the beginning of 1854 there were 125 slaves. These were divided into a domestic staff comprising a butler, two waiters, four housemaids, a nurse, a laundress, a seamstress, a dairy maid, and a gardener; in the fields were plowmen, hoe hands, wagoners, and ox drivers, with two cooks to look after them; in addition, there were a carriage driver, a hostler, a stable boy, a shepherd, a cowherd, and a hog herd. Also on the inventory were several skilled mechanics employed entirely by the plantation. These included two carpenters and five stone-masons, a miller, two blacksmiths, two shoemakers, five women spinners, and one woman weaver. (Some owners also had their own coopers who were kept busy drawing staves and hoop poles and making barrels; cotton was baled, of course, but most plantations had plenty of use for barrels and hogsheads.) Such a listing did not count children, old men, and women. This assortment of workers is fairly typical.

In a moderately sized place, the rows of slave cabins (known as "the street") would all be near the "big house," but on large estates they were likely to be more distant, near the overseer's house, the smithy, and the stables, with corncribs and wagon sheds nearby. The house-servants' cabins were near the master's house, as were the office, the schoolroom, the dairy and laundry, the smokehouse, the well, and the open-air laundry. It was here that any other buildings for craftsmen were likely to be located—weaving sheds, for instance, where textiles were spun and woven for many household uses.

Missing on the plantation were such sophisticated crafts as silversmithing, engraving, gilding, and the like, but most of the other crafts found in town could also be encountered in the country, where practically all the necessities of life were supplied locally by a slave. There was, of course, less specialization than in the cities. A carpenter probably did his own joinery, and he might very well be called upon to make furniture as well—from the simplest of tables and chairs, for slave or porch use, to beautiful pieces for the master's parlor or bedroom. In his spare time, he might amuse himself by making doll furniture for a child or a "cunjer" stick for himself. The wainwright was his own wheelwright, and the blacksmith did farrier's work, too. He might be called upon to make anything from a wrought-iron gate to a kitchen pot.

In the city, specific patterns were likely to be followed, and the work had to conform to what was in style. But plantation needs were simple, and most articles were made with use, rather than beauty, in mind, though beauty often did result. In the country, a master would be more likely to describe in general what he wanted and leave the details to the slave. The learning process in the country also differed somewhat from that in the city. Techniques were taught under an apprentice system here, too, but it more closely resembled the African variety. Some crafts, such as basket-making, sewing, weaving, or net-making, were taught exactly as in Africa by adults to children in an informal way. Also, as in African society, particular skills were apt to remain in one family on the plantations. A son would be assigned as an assistant to his craftsman father and trained to take over the work after his death. Probably the slaves themselves encouraged this, teaching their children bits and pieces of their trade until they were old enough to be recommended to the master as apprentices. By making the youngster more valuable, the father reduced the danger of the son's being sold away to another master. Additionally, it was a system he was accustomed to, since, as we have seen, the crafts in Africa for the most part were kept in one family.

If a planter lacked some particular craftsman and felt the need warranted it, the most likely youngster on the plantation would be "bound out" as an indentured apprentice to some city craftsman for the usual five to seven years, and then returned to the country. His worth to his owner would have increased tenfold. If there were not enough work to keep a craftsman busy on the plantation all year round, he could be hired out to neighboring planters for a handy profit. For instance, when Springfield plantation, in South Carolina,

Slave-made doll's chair. Coin added to indicate scale. (Collection Old Slave Mart Museum, Photo, author)

Early engraving showing an elderly slave whittling toys on the porch of "The Big House." (New York Public Library Picture Collection)

St. Andrew's Church, Prairieville, Ala. (Old Slave Mart Museum Picture Collection. Photo, Scott)

House-servants' quarters with slave-made pantile roof at Boone Hall Plantation, S.C. (Photo, author)

Detail of pantiles, showing S shape. (Collection Old Slave Mart Museum. Photo, author)

Detail of construction by slave craftsmen. Left cross-section of original beams from Ryan's Mart (about 1820), now The Old Slave Mart Museum, showing tenoned ends. Right, lath showing plaster molded around and locked in back. (Collection Old Slave Mart Museum. Photo, author)

was built under the direction of Master Carpenter Champlin, Negro artisans were hired from planters in the neighborhood. The plantation accounts read: "By hire, of one of Maj. S. Porcher's Carpenters @ $20 per month, being with me for the good of Champlin. $140." Planters who hired out slaves in this way received the slave's wages and were saved the expense of feeding him while at work. The slave craftsman received no pay, but some planters supplied their hired slaves with rations of rum.

Planters also used their slaves for various community services, such as helping to build a church or aiding a neighbor in time of trouble. For instance, when fire destroyed the house of John Sims at Gippy Plantation, South Carolina, it was rebuilt by Negro artisans lent by sympathetic neighbors. And St. Andrew's Episcopal Church in Prairieville, Alabama, was constructed entirely by slaves belonging to members of the congregation. They worked under the direction of Peter Lee and Joe Glascow, two master carpenters who were slaves of Captain Henry A. Tayloe. This beautiful little church was consecrated in 1859 and stands today exactly as it was built. The Gothic exterior is painted a red-brown color, and the interior is reached through large double doors hung on massive iron hinges that were hand-wrought in a plantation forge. William M. Spencer, church historian, gives this further description:

> A stain brewed from the stems of tobacco plants was applied to the interior wood walls; although nothing has been done since to this woodwork, it is in an excellent state of preservation and has a pleasing and mellowed appearance. The symbols and figures on the altar rail and elsewhere in the chancel were carved expertly and beautifully by Peter Lee. . . .

Negro craftsmen also built the utility buildings and slave quarters on the plantations. And in many cases all the materials were made right on the place. Trees were felled and sawed into lumber; shingles were made of pine or cypress with the aid of an instrument called a froe, a splitting tool with a thick, wedge-shaped blade. It was driven downward along the grain of the wood and was also utilized by the cooper for riving out barrel staves.

House tiles and bricks were often made right on the plantation. Some of the early bricks were brought over from England as ship's ballast, but the supply was insufficient to meet the demands of the expanding colonies, and brick-making developed early. Some of the bricks were sun dried, some fired in a kiln. Colonial bricks were generally much larger than English ones and varied from "Savannah gray" in Georgia to various shades of red and brown. The tiles used in Charleston were sometimes imported from Great Britain and sometimes made locally, either in town or on the outlying plantations. They were generally of two sorts, unglazed—of a very attractive salmon pink—and glazed, which were a dark, almost purplish, hue.

Construction of the "big house" was, of course, more elaborate than that of the other plantation buildings, and it was usually designed by an architect. Sometimes the plantation owner merged his own ideas with those of the housewright, which gave him the satisfaction of having a house that was distinctively his own.

Although the basic designs for these houses usually originated in Europe, American adaptations were often simplified and refined in line and proportion. Most Americans had little patience with the frills and furbelows so dear to the hearts of European society, where tastes were set by royalty. While they wanted reminders of the Old World, they were well satisfied with more practical renditions.

Sometimes the housewright worked without plans, even though he had designed the building; sometimes pattern books were used as guides. The work of European designers such as Palladio, the Italian, and Robert Adam, the Englishman, exercised great influence on colonial architects and cabinetmakers. But even when the American craftsman (black or white) used a pattern book in order to follow the prevailing mode, he changed or modified his design to conform to his own or his employer's personal tastes and ideas. In this respect he was similar to the African woodcarver who followed certain basic rules in fashioning a mask, yet had plenty of scope for individuality and variation. Thus, American designs were refreshingly new and original and not copies or exact reproductions of older ones.

Some master builders gave their joiners and plasterers drawings to follow, but many of the housewright's artisans worked from a general description and had considerable latitude for interpretation. But regardless of the design or the builder, most of the men involved in building a plantation house were probably Negroes—whether owned by the housewright or the planter, or hired from neighbors.

Work on such houses called for consummate skill. Joiners often did woodcarving on mantels, pilasters, pediments, or moldings. Many of the delicate architectural details that appear to be woodcarvings, however, are in reality plaster or putty that has been modeled in sculptural fashion. Workers in these materials were called stucco workers or plasterers. Negroes were, and still are, particularly skilled at this work.

Even the more mundane tasks of housebuilding were done with great care. Beams were "mortised and tenoned"—notched and fitted together and held by pegs instead of nails. Plaster was not applied merely to the surface of lath, but molded around the lath until it locked in back. Treated in this way, the plaster has survived for hundreds of years. The plaster itself was often made of oyster-shell lime (crushed oyster shells and sand), which is practically indestructible. Laths were split from both cypress and pine and allowed to season for as long as ten years before being used.

It is difficult to say which was the most important of the plantation craftsmen, the carpenter or the blacksmith. The latter made the various pieces of hardware necessary to complete the work of the carpenter; nails, screws, bolts, locks, keys, hinges, shutter hooks, and pipe supports were all handforged by the blacksmith. He made tools and agricultural implements of various sorts, including hedge clippers, tin snips, bale hooks, mattocks, hoes, mule snubbers and bits; also rice testers, sugar dippers, bathtubs, and various kinds of weights. Some did farrier's work as well. And, if he were particularly skilled, he might be called upon to design and make a wrought-iron gate or balcony for his master.

The names of slave blacksmiths, like those of their white counterparts, are usually unknown, but here and there the reputation or work of a particular craftsman has survived through oral tradition, or as a family heirloom. For instance, a most interesting and shapely set of andirons representing Adam and Eve was wrought by an old plantation slave on Silk Hope Plantation in South Carolina, and is still cherished by a descendant of the planter who commissioned it.

Beautiful Adam-style plasterwork from the stairway of the Dock Street Theater, Charleston, S.C. About 1802. (Photo, Emmett Robinson)

Hedge clippers made by a slave blacksmith at Fenwick Hall, John's Island, S.C., and a heavy garden tool that is a cross between a hoe and a pitchfork. (Collection Old Slave Mart Museum. Photo, author)

Top to bottom: Pee weight (block shape) used for weighing cotton. A recess in the bottom held lead to measure fractions of the weight of the pee. Copper rice tester, plunged into the depths of a full barrel of rice to test quality to determine grade and price. It is similar to African *Po* spoons shown on page 47. Mule snubber, used to lock mule's jaw to prevent him from biting the farrier while being shod. (Collection Old Slave Mart Museum. Photo, author)

Various hinges made by slave blacksmiths. (Collection, Old Slave Mart Museum. Photo, author)

Pair of wrought-iron andirons from Mt. Hope Plantation, S.C. (Courtesy, Mrs. Samuel Lapham. Photo, author)

Secretary from the James Hurt Shorter plantation at Summerville, Ala. About 1850. (Courtesy, Mr. Edward Shorter)

Just as the blacksmith was often an artist, the carpenter combined the duties of joiner, woodcarver, and cabinetmaker as well. It is difficult to tell exactly how many slaves practiced the art of cabinetmaking, inasmuch as the owners were taxed according to their slaves' particular trades; it is thought that many of them were listed as "carpenters" in order to avoid the higher tax required for "cabinetmakers." For instance, the 1864 inventory of Dr. Robert Harllee lists 116 slaves on his extensive plantation, Melrose, at Mars Bluff, South Carolina. Two of these were called "carpenters," but they were highly skilled craftsmen who made many of Melrose's beautiful pieces of furniture, which are still treasured by Dr. Harllee's grandchildren. One of these items was originally a built-in cupboard or china cabinet so large it had to be cut in half in order to remove it from the house. Beautifully made of pine grown on the plantation, it is a piece to be proud of, and certainly the maker was not a mere carpenter. Dr. Harllee's slaves also made tables, corner cabinets, bureaus, and washstands.

Another excellent cabinetmaker was a man by the name of Ned, who was owned in the 1840s by James Benson Zachry, near Covington, Georgia. Ned made many fine pieces, including a china cabinet or bookcase now owned by one of Mr. Zachry's descendants. The shelves are made of single planks of irregular thickness, indicating hand-planing; the back was also hand-planed. All the corners are wood-pegged, but hand-forged screws, nails, and hinges are used elsewhere. Although the frame is of pine, the molding is poplar and the door panels are walnut. Chippendale had made mahogany a popular wood for furniture in America, but on the plantations, as on northern farms, home-grown woods were more often used; among these were pine, walnut, and fruitwoods; in the South there was tulipwood, usually called poplar but actually a magnolia.

James Hurt Shorter, of Summerville, Alabama, owned a slave craftsman who, by tradition, made several pieces of furniture for various members of the family. Among them was a single spool bed that once graced the lovely antebellum home of the Fontaines in Columbus, Georgia. The bed has since disappeared, but one example of this cabinetmaker's work, an exceptionally handsome and skillfully made mahogany secretary with carved wood handles and solid doors, is still highly prized by Edward Shorter of Columbus.

Other notable pieces of slave-made furniture authenticated by oral and written family histories include a mahogany bureau at Green Bollo, Mississippi; a captain's chair in Montgomery, Alabama; a bureau and a pair of ottomans made by slaves in a plantation cabinetshop on the estate of Ephraim Clayton, in West Asheville, North Carolina. The ottomans are quite elegant, with handcarved legs, and were originally covered with black broadcloth embroidered in red silk thread: there were red roses on one and red poppies on the other.

As was typical of American design during the period, the examples of slave cabinetmaking were simpler than their European prototypes, though they did call for some embellishments that had to be laboriously handcarved into the wood. Some of the furniture made on the plantation is so plain as to seem stark in its simplicity. Yet, simple though it may be, it is undeniably beautiful. As Edwin Tunis says in *Colonial Craftsmen:* "Obviously, it isn't the wood that gives quality to furniture, and it isn't the polished surface. It is, first, good proportions and precise shaping of visible parts like moldings and legs; next it is in the perfect fitting of invisible joinings and the use of the right kind of joint for each purpose." These slave-made pieces no doubt benefited from the African's propensity to retain beauty through balance and proportion

Furniture from Melrose, plantation of Dr. Robert Harllee (1807-1872). (Courtesy, Mrs. W. G. Wallace. Photos, Sonny Smith)

One of two pine side tables with mahogany knobs on the drawers. Joins made with pegs.

Slave-made pine bureau with beaded mirror to match.

Corner whatnot made of pine and varnished a mahogany color.

China cabinet. Once a built-in cupboard, it was cut in half. The door has been reversed; the lack of a cornice on the upper right-hand corner shows where the division was made.

Captain's chair with claw handgrips. (Courtesy, Mr. Paul B. Fuller, Montgomery, Ala. Photo, Scott)

One of a pair of Walnut ottoman, made by slaves in the plantation cabinet-shop of Ephram Clayton (1804–1892), West Ashville, N.C. (Courtesy, Miss Julia Adelaide Clayton, Photo, Sonny Smith)

Corner china cabinet from Mt. Hope Plantation. Like most "pineland" furniture it is starkly simple, but beautiful. (Courtesy, Mrs. Samuel Lapham. Photo, author)

and interacting tensions while reducing his design to its ultimate simplicity.

An example of this is the desk made by a slave on The Elms Plantation near Millbrook, Alabama. It is a type often used in plantation offices by the master. In the office, the master, if he were a conscientious planter and not an absentee owner or a dilettante, worked over the plantation accounts and record books, all laboriously kept in longhand. It was a business office in every sense of the word, and its furniture was utilitarian. Nevertheless, even such pieces are quite beautiful.

Other examples of this simplicity in design can be found in the furnishings of South Carolina's summer houses in the interior "pinelands," where, to escape the muggy heat and malaria of the coastal regions, many white families moved during the hottest months. While city houses were furnished with sophisticated furniture made by professional cabinetmakers or imported from England, these summer homes, whether on plantations or not, were more simply supplied with slave-made furniture of indigenous wood. This pineland furniture, as it is called, is more nearly akin to early colonial in New England, or even to Danish modern, than it is to Chippendale or Hepplewhite.

Many plantations, while not maintaining an actual cabinetshop, had slaves who just built whatever was needed. Such items might include a built-in china closet for the butler's pantry or a large built-in bookcase or cupboard. When Dr. Harllee's daughter, Louisa, was married, he had his slave build her a washstand as a wedding present. On the grounds of the estate, Dr. Harllee and his slave cabinetmaker chose the walnut tree from which it was made. Similarly, when Samuel MacDonald Carter of Carter's Quarters, in northern Georgia, wanted a couch on which to take his afternoon naps, he insisted on selecting the particular tree from which his slave carpenter made an exceptionally lovely sleigh bed. It is single-bed width and was furnished with rope "springs" and a feather-bed mattress. This bed was in use until ten years ago, when Mr. Carter's granddaughter, Mrs. Crowell, donated it to the Georgia Historical Society. According to Mrs. Crowell, there were several slave cabinetmakers at Carter's Quarters, under the direction of an older slave who was a master of the craft. They made many pieces of furniture still cherished by Mrs. Crowell, including a heavy walnut lamp table and a walnut chest of drawers.

Plantation craftsmen also supplied the slave cabins, porches, and gardens with furniture of a less finished type than that made for the master's house. Take, for instance, the chairs made by a slave named Sutton, in Camden, South Carolina. Born with a club foot, he was taught the art of chair-making because it could be done in a seated position. Astraddle a special workbench and using drawknives, he painstakingly shaped the subtle curves necessary for the rockers and other chair parts. This resulted in strong plantation chairs, that were stained green. Destined for porch or servants' quarters, they were well proportioned, with graceful backs shaped to fit the contours of the body.

Sutton always twisted and wove corn shucks for the seats; his use of natural fibers is reminiscent of Africa. The use of corn shucks for chair seats, as well as for floor mats, was common among southern Negroes until very recently. The technique may have been handed down from one generation to another from some remote African ancestor. Today it is almost impossible to find such articles, because the modern method of harvesting corn chops the shucks into bits and makes them useless for weaving.

On many large plantations, clothing the slaves was no mean task. Although some owners allowed their household servants to wear cast-offs and the field

Marble-topped wash stand from Melrose. Made by a slave cabinetmaker from a specially selected walnut tree on Dr. Harllee's plantation, for his daughter, Louisa, in 1848. (SECO photo, Joe Nesbitt)

Walnut sleigh bed, for napping. Made by slave cabinetmaker at Carter's Quarters. Slave-made quilt. (Courtesy, Georgia Historical Commission. Photo, Forrest)

Plantation rocker made by Sutton, with woven corn shuck seat. (Collection Old Slave Mart Museum. Photo, M. B. Wilson)

Chair made by Sutton, a slave. Seat and doormat in foreground are woven of corn shucks. (Collection Old Slave Mart Museum. Photo, author)

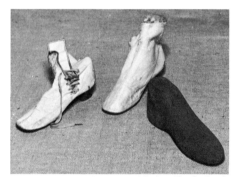

Wedding shoes made on a straight last like the hand-carved one beside them. Right and left shoes as we know them were not introduced until 1860. (Collection Old Slave Mart Museum. Photo, Phillips)

hands to go in tatters, the records show that most of the large plantations made regular allotments of clothing to both. James H. Hammond's plantation manual calls for the following clothing allowances: for each man, in the fall, two cotton shirts, a pair of woolen pants, and a woolen jacket, and in the spring two cotton shirts and two pair of cotton pants; for each woman, six yards of woolen cloth and six yards of cotton cloth in the fall, six yards of light and six of heavy cotton cloth in the spring, with needles, thread, and buttons on each occasion. Each worker was to have a stout pair of shoes in the fall (except for house-servants, many slaves went barefoot in the summer) and a heavy blanket every third year.

There was always a big demand for those skilled as "spinsters" (i.e., women who could spin thread) or "weavers," and they brought high prices on the slave market. Not every plantation, however, made its own cloth, and those that did often supplemented homespun with "boughten" goods.

Shoes were also bought occasionally, but if possible they were made right on the place. Blankets for the "big house," as well as for slaves, were handmade, as were sheets, bedspreads, quilts, and many articles of dress.

The Huguenots, French Protestant immigrants, carried their knowledge of textile-making into the South and found many Afro-American slaves already skilled in this art. In many parts of Africa, however, it is the men who weave; in America it is always a "woman's task," so many of the weavers had to be taught how to do it.

Nearly every plantation of any size had a weaving room, where the mistress of the house trained her slaves to spin and weave. Until 1785, only handweaving was known. An interesting description of such a room has come to us from Tennessee, where Mrs. James Stuart Pilcher recalled that, in her home in 1850:

There were two looms in the loom-room, and two Negro women were kept busy all the time weaving; there were eight or ten others who did nothing but spin cotton and woolen thread; others spooled and reeled it into hanks. The spinning was all done on the large wheel, from the raw cotton; a corn-shuck was wrapped tightly around the steel spindle, then the thread was run and spun on this shuck until it was full; then these were reeled off into hanks of thread, then spooled on to corn-cobs with holes burned through them. These were placed in an upright frame, with long slender rods of hickory wood something like a ramrod run through them. The frame held about one hundred of these cob-spools; the end of the cotton thread from each spool was gathered up by an experienced warper who carried all the threads back and forth on the large warping-bars . . . These women spun and wove all the clothing worn by the Negroes on the plantation; cotton cloth for women and men in the summer time; and jeans for the men; linsey-woolsey for the women and children for winter. All were well clothed.

Most American weavers followed the European customs of recording patterns by a system of written notation; these "drafts," as weavers call them, passed from hand to hand as long as the paper on which they were done lasted. Whether the Afro-American slaves adopted the European draft or worked without one, as is done in Africa and in the United States by Navajo Indian weavers, is not known. In any case, the looms used by the slaves resembled African ones, and the slaves adapted to any differences quickly.

Homespun cloth for the Negroes was known and sold as "Virginia Cloth," or "Negro cloth," but slaves made textiles for white people as well. Much homespun, handwoven clothing was worn right up to the end of the Civil War. Governor Lucas of South Carolina had helped to establish a domestic textile industry in this country as early as 1785 when he sent two Irish servants, a weaver and a spinner, to his daughter, Eliza Lucas Pinckney, instructing her to apprentice Negro women to them "to learn to spin, and wheels to be made for them." These women, and hundreds of others like them, learned to spin well, and excellent cloth was woven in South Carolina up to the twentieth century.

Thomas Jefferson wrote in 1786 that in the "four southernmost States the poor are almost entirely clothed with . . . homespun cotton," and a vast quantity of homespun cloth was made annually on Virginia plantations, thousands of yards a year at Mount Vernon alone for slave-wear and for the mistress of the house as well.

Perhaps because clothes go out of style and are discarded, while bedspreads, quilts, and coverlets do not, more of the latter have survived as examples of slave handweaving.

The coverlet patterns were similar to those of African textiles, but this was no doubt the result of the similarity of the looms rather than of any direct influence of African culture. Most slave-made coverlets appear to be common American designs, but some do not adhere strictly to the traditional patterns. They seem to be adaptations or variations of them, as though some scope for originality were allowed, just as there is some latitude in the making of African crafts within the traditional rules. (One unusual spread, for instance, is particularly interesting. It is more like contemporary "op art" than like the usual European patterns, or, for that matter, African designs.) But if the Afro-American slave had to learn European patterns to please her mistress, she apparently did so quickly.

Each of the common patterns had a name, but all of them varied with the locality. One might be called by one name in one state, but given an entirely different name in another. Size also affected the name. Pine Bloom, in Kentucky, became known as Gentlemen's Fancy, Sea Star, or Isle of Patmos when woven on an enlarged scale. Catalpa Flower was also called Work Complete or Lady's Fancy, depending on the state where it was made. One reason weavers gave different descriptive names to the same coverlet pattern may be that the patterns seem to change, depending on how you look at them. For instance, in spite of their dissimilarities, both Pine Bloom and Catalpa Flower could just as easily have been called Chariot Wheels, the popular name for a circle with two intersecting diameters.

Look at the patterns illustrated for any length of time and they change before your eyes. The crossed diameters in Chariot Wheels can be followed through an entire spread until it appears to have a diamond pattern. Yet in another moment, one sees only the wheels. Blocks and squares appear one moment and disappear the next, as the eye picks out and notices some other line or shape—first the light and then the dark. The Cross changes into Snail's Trail when viewed at an angle. Optical illusions are created when the spreads are seen from a distance, too. In fact, to the connoisseur these old coverlets have all the fascination of contemporary "op art."

Most old coverlets were woven in two strips that were seamed down the center to make them wide enough to cover a bed. These seams are one way of determing the age of such spreads: the lack of seaming indicates a later date. Sometimes slave-made spreads are seamed with no apparent attempt to match the pattern. In view of the obvious skill of the weavers, this was probably done deliberately. Often slaves refused to plow a straight furrow or follow a

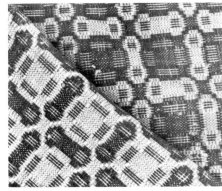

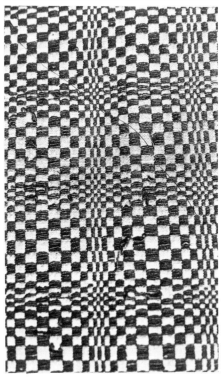

Top: detail of single-weave bedspread, white cotton ground threads overshot with indigo-dyed wool. Woven by a slave near Macon, Ga., in pattern called Catalpa Flower. Shown folded over, the reversal of pattern on the other side can be seen. Center: detail of homespun blue and white coverlet, in Pine Bloom pattern, handwoven by a slave at Laurel Hill Plantation, James River, Va., in 1800. Note that the light areas on each side are dark on the other. Bottom: detail of bedspread woven by slaves on one of the Lovelace Plantations near LaGrange, Ga. It appears to be an original design. The complementary colors of blue and orange buff add to the dazzling "op art" effect of this spread. (Collection Old Slave Mart. Photos author)

Detail of a quilt at Vann House, Ga. (see page 85). In this patchwork quilt, the stitches follow the outline of the design, which was usually floral in this kind of quilt. (Courtesy, Georgia Historical Commission. Photo, Forrest)

Slave-made piecework quilt in a fan pattern from the home of Sidney Lanier, Georgia poet. (Collection Old Slave Mart Museum. Photo, author)

straight line in a pattern without occasionally deviating to foil the malevolent spirits. When they walked down a country road, especially at night, a quick jog to right or left served the same purpose. Considered supersitions by slave-owners, these practices were remnants of African religious beliefs, clung to by people denied complete acculturation in America.

Most of the coverlets were woven of cotton and wool, which were quite common fibers on southern plantations. Linen was more rare, and silk was restricted to very limited areas. Flax culture was more usual in the North, but a few southern planters raised it in small quantities for their own use.

Most of the sheep were raised merely for personal use, and the wool was sheared, carded, and spun in order to weave it into cloth for the plantation. Cotton, on the other hand, was a money crop, and so was silk. Many people are unaware of the fact that silk production ever took place in America, but in fact it did. When the Huguenots began settling in South Carolina in the 1680s, it was hoped they could make the wine, oil, and silk for which England sent so much gold across the Channel.

In 1699, Sir Nathaniel Johnson was the first to begin raising silk in commercial quantities on his South Carolina plantation, Silk Hope, where he had planted more than 500,000 mulberry trees. Negro children were employed in feeding the silkworms, and, as late as 1824, advertisements appeared in the Charleston *Courier* offering to buy Negroes who understood silkworm culture and the unwinding of cocoons. Slaves also wove silk for Martha Washington. She is said to have carefully dyed all her worn-out silk gowns and silk scraps to a desired shade, raveled them with care, and had her slaves weave them into chair- or cushion covers. Once she reversed the process, for she showed some visitors a dress of red and white striped material—the white was cotton, but the red was made of raveled chair covers and silk from the General's worn-out stockings!

The colors used in the old textiles came from many sources. Areas near ports made much use of imported colorings: madder (red) and camwood from South America, fustic (yellow) from the West Indies, turmeric (yellow) from the East Indies, tin from Cornwall, cochineal (red) from Mexico, and woad (blue) from England; but most of the colors were obtained from local materials. The study of homemade dyes is fascinating. Many trees, such as hickory, walnut, maple, chestnut, butternut, black oak, and sage, and flowers such as the lowly black-eyed Susan, were magically transformed into glowing colors, with or without the use of mordants, or fixers. In 1863, a list of dyes indigenous to the southern states was drawn up by Francis Pyre Porcher, a surgeon, and published in Charleston, South Carolina. It included no less than thirty-nine different varieties of wild plants, among them many familiar ones like common nettle, laurel, burdock, clematis, sassafras, larkspur, cocklebur, alder, cypress, and wild indigo.

Indigo, used for many woven coverlets and Negro cloth, was first introduced into America in the eighteenth century by a South Carolina girl, Eliza Lucas, but it did not become popular here until war with France forced English weavers, who previously obtained the dye from the French, to look elsewhere, and gave the South Carolina low country the incentive to cultivate it. Thereafter it became one of the region's biggest export crops and was also used domestically.

Aside from weaving, another important task for women slaves was making quilts or comforters. Quilts, which refer to two or more fabrics held together with many tiny stitches, fall into two general groups—the "pieced work" and the "patchwork," or "laid on." Quiltmakers argue hotly over which is older, more difficult, or more beautiful. The striking difference between the two is that in pieced work small scraps of cloth are sewn together to form the patterned top, whereas in patchwork the design is appliquéd on a solid cloth background. Beautiful and skillful examples of both types can be found.

An old saying says, "A patch is a sure sign of poverty," and the average person might imagine a patchwork quilt to be made of leftover scraps patched together helter-skelter and used for economy's sake. Such quilts were made but were called crazy quilts, and they were not introduced until the late Victorian period. A patchwork quilt, on the other hand, had no association with poverty. To make a patchwork quilt, the edges of tiny "patches" of colored cloth were turned under and attached with minute hemming stitches to the fabric that formed the background. This "appliqué," or "applied" work, is known to have been made by the early Egyptians and rose to a high art in Europe, where it was used on the banners of the crusaders. As has been mentioned, striking appliquéd banners or wall hangings have long been made in Dahomey.

In a piecework quilt each integral part of the pattern is a separate piece of material joined to the next part by a running stitch that makes a seam on the wrong side. Although these quilts were often made of bits and pieces of discarded or worn-out clothes, they were always carefully matched for color and design, and sometimes specially purchased fabrics were added to the scraps.

Quilting, a separate art, was born of a need to protect against bitter cold and was used for garments and wall hangings. It was first practiced in Europe by the peasantry and later became a courtly art, when the term "quilt" was also given to the stitched, wadded lining for body armor. In America, usage has restricted the word so that now it is applied only to a lightweight, closely stitched bedcover, usually with an interlining of cotton or wool batting.

Once the top cover of the quilt was completed, whether by patching or by piecing, the process of quilting proceeded in the same way for both. The back, or lining, was cut from some lightweight material (usually white cotton), and then the quilt was "ready for the frames." The frame consisted of four narrow pieces of wood, two somewhat longer than the quilt and two shorter, with holes bored in the ends of each piece. The pieces were held together at each corner with clamps, so the corners made true right angles. As a rule the frames rested on chair backs, and each side bar was wrapped with sturdy tape or ticking to which was tacked the edges of the lining, one side to each bar. The extra length was rolled up on one side of the frame, which was securely fastened and the cloth stretched in both directions. On this stretched lining the cotton or wool batting used for interlining was carefully and smoothly spread, then the pieced or patched top was placed on it and basted to the edge of the lining. Great care was required to keep all edges true and to stretch all parts of the quilt uniformly.

The quilting pattern was usually drawn, although "quilting by the eye" was common. Where straight lines were involved, chalk-coated strings stretched tightly at the desired intervals, then held up and snapped smartly down on the quilt, would leave a faint chalk line to guide the needle. Carved wooden blocks, heavily chalked, served for more intricate patterns, though a saucer or plate could be used to form a perfect circle or arc for simple designs. Quilting varied from simple diagonals to exceedingly elaborate patterns. Among the most popular were designs resembling ostrich feathers, shells, and twisted rope, as well as the fan pattern.

The quilting was done with fine cotton thread, and the running stitch that

Hand-forged quilting clamps, made by a slave blacksmith. Used to hold quilts to a frame. Lanier quilt is in the Log Cabin design and quilted in a hanging diamond pattern on a very early sewing machine. (Collection Old Slave Mart Museum. Photo, author)

Hand-tufted slave-made piecework quilt in Eight-Pointed Star design. (Collection Old Slave Mart Museum. Photo, author)

White counterpane woven by slaves on a loom from about 1800. Handmade lace edge. (Courtesy, Alabama Department of Archives and History. Photo, Scott)

Pantalette leg, hand-embroidered by a slave. (Collection Old Slave Mart Museum. Photo, author)

Tucked petticoat, made in 1840 by Old Aunt Sarah, a slave who was a household seamstress. Note the tiny stitches and mathematically precise tucking. The trim may be Swiss embroidery. (Collection Old Slave Mart Museum. Photo, author)

Dolls made for white children by a slave named Emmaline. Boy doll (1850) is hand-knitted. "Mammy" doll (1882) is dressed partly in buttons and materials from Emmaline's clothes. (Collection Old Slave Mart Museum. Photo, author)

was used had to be as small and even as possible. This was not easy, especially since the quilt's two thicknesses of cloth and interlining of cotton were stretched so tightly that it was difficult to push the needle through. As a result, quilters became dexterous in overcoming the difficulties of their work. Some quilters preferred to insert the needle in two separate motions—one up and one down; others used a running stitch. Some liked a straight needle, while others treasured their bent ones.

The quilter was unable to reach more than twelve inches conveniently, so after a strip of this width had been completed along the entire length of the coverlet, this portion was rolled up on the bar of the frame and an equal amount was unrolled from the other side. This new section was then marked for quilting and again quilted as far as the seamstress could reach. This process was continued until the entire piece was finished, after which it was removed from the frame and the edges bound with bias material. Since the stitching went through to the other side, the entire pattern was repeated on the lining, so the back also had a pattern in low relief.

Designs might be common ones used throughout the colonies and states, or each individual seamstress could create her own. They were handed down through several generations and often traveled from one locality to another by way of the peddler who stayed overnight and brought news or swapped gossip and patterns. Each of the patterns had its own name; many were of political origin. One, for instance, was the Log Cabin design, which has been popular since the days of "Tippecanoe and Tyler Too."

Quilts were padded with raw cotton, and before the invention of the cotton gin, female slaves were given the task of picking out the seeds. Nothing but handpicked cotton went into the best southern quilts. This was not always true of northern quilts. In many of the latter, the seeds may be seen quite plainly if the quilt is held up to the light.

Some quilts were tufted. Tufting was a technique used to prevent the batting from slipping, and it was employed only in the thickest of quilts (or comforters) because they could not be punctured easily with a needle for quilting.

Slaves who showed a talent for needlework were trained to do all sorts of delicate tasks, such as tatting, embroidery, macramé, lace, knitting, and dressmaking, as well as quilting and weaving. Many examples of their work still survive. There are for instance, tatted lace; hand-embroidered petticoats, wedding handkerchiefs, and pantalette legs; and tucked taffeta skirts. The tucks are mathematically precise and the stitches are so tiny they can hardly be seen. One lovely slave-made quilt that was once the property of the southern poet, Sidney Lanier, was quilted on an early sewing machine. Already skilled in the use of the needle, slave women easily adapted themselves to the sewing machine, which was developed first by Walter Hunt (inventor of the safety pin and fountain pen) and patented in 1846 by Elias Howe.

The women's tasks, like those of the men, often overlapped. Emmaline, a slave purchased in 1850 at the age of fourteen by a Mr. Montgomery, first served Mrs. Montgomery as a personal servant, and was later a nurse for her fourteen children. But she also did weaving and sewing, and in 1882 she made two dolls for the Montgomery grandchildren. One is a hand-knitted boy doll; the other is a "mammy" doll wearing an African-style bandanna, or headtie, and dressed in bits and pieces of Emmaline's own clothes, including an embroidered collar and jet buttons.

Aside from needlework and weaving, one other household task of great importance was assigned to the women. This was the making of candles for use on the plantation. The first fine candles used in South Carolina were imported from England, although a cheap variety, tallow dip, was also made locally of tallow and fat from cattle and game. But as the settlers searched meadows and woods for materials to make candles, excellent American substitutes were found. Myrtlewood, or bayberry, yielded a fragrant green wax. Candles of bayberry were more expensive than tallow but cheaper than wax and they were highly prized because, unlike other candles, they did not melt in hot weather. Bees were kept as much for their wax as for their honey, and even the waxy berries from cedar trees were used. In the eighteenth century spermaceti, from sperm whales, was introduced, and a candle made of this produced more light than three tallow candles.

Local materials, however, appear to have predominated in South Carolina. Hampton and El Dorado Plantations on the South Santee River were noted for their myrtleberry candles. At Hampton the household arts of "Maum Patty," the Negro housekeeper of colonial times, were passed down from mother to daughter for five generations; the slaves took entire charge of the candle-making.

Usually candles were made outdoors because of the danger of fire, but sometimes they were made in the second kitchen, also used for cake- and jelly-making, or in one of the separate outhouses. Loosely spun hemp, tow, and cotton, and sometimes even milkweed silk, were twisted to make wicks.

Three standard methods were employed: beeswax candles were pressed into shape around a wick, but the two methods employed in making tallow candles were used for all other types of wax. They were either run into tin molds, like those illustrated, or dipped. For dipped candles, six or eight carefully straightened wicks were suspended from candle rods, usually wooden sticks or poles, and each rod with its row of wicks was dipped in turn into a great kettle of boiling water and tallow, with time to cool and harden between dips. A good worker could make two hundred candles in a day. When molds were used, each wick was attached to a wire or nail placed across the open top of the cylinder and drawn through the hole in the bottom. Melted tallow was poured carefully around the wicks, the candles were allowed to harden, and then they were removed. Slaves were usually allowed four candles a week for their own use.

The kitchen, of course, provided many types of work, both for men and women, not only in the art of cooking, but in hand-making the various utensils needed. Most of the cooking was done over an open fireplace, which lacked any method for adjusting the heat. Distance from the flame was the only determinant. So the blacksmith had to supply the cook with a trammel—a notched gadget on which the pots could be hung at varying heights above a fire. He also made numerous kinds of pots, some of which were for cooking "grits" (a corruption of the word "grist", the ground corn fresh from the grist mill) or "hominy" (as it was called after it was cooked); iron pots to set on the coals; dippers and spoons. Mortars and pestles also were a vital necessity, and they were made of various materials, often by slave craftsmen. The most common were marble, used for medicines; granite or bronze, used for crushing crystalized cane sugar for the master's family; and iron, used for the same purpose by the slaves.

Humble and tedious though most of these tasks may seem to us today, the Afro-American slave brought to them that same pride of craftsmanship and creative power that had characterized his African ancestor. And, as President Leopold Senghor of Senegal has said, "This is the original trademark of art."

Candle molds made by a South Carolina plantation tinsmith. (Collection Old Slave Mart Museum. Photo, author)

Slave-made unglazed pottery jar, a rare example of this fragile craft. (Collection Old Slave Mart Museum. Photo, author)

Left-handed copper dipper made by a Negro blacksmith. Used in making sugar, it has a double lip that holds back the scum as syrup is poured into molds. (Collection Old Slave Mart Museum. Photo, author)

Slave-made trunk, about 1780. Covered with rawhide and lined with patterned paper: hand-forged iron bands form the hinges in back and part of the locking system in front. (Collection Old Slave Mart Museum. Photo, author)

# 6  THE PIONEER ARTISTS

*Caroline Loguen* by William Simpson; about 1854.
(Permanent Collection, Howard University Gallery of
Art)

Until recently, many Negroes thought they had little reason for pride in their heritage. This attitude is expressed by James Baldwin, in *Notes of A Native Son:* "not that I liked black people; in fact, I despised them, possibly because they had no Rembrandt." Yet, even if there were no Rembrandts among them, black artists of whom Afro-Americans can be justly proud abounded in the past. Aside from the myriad anonymous artists, from Nok to Charleston, we even know a few by name. One of the earliest was Ighu-igha, Benin's brass-smith, still revered as patron saint of the craft; and there are many others, among them the pioneer artists in America. Yet the latter seldom, if ever, find their way into traditional art history books. This is not necessarily a deliberate omission of Negro artists as a group. Rather, it is the failure of art historians to evaluate the contributions of black artists within the context of their background and opportunities. These black artists are outstanding when judged by the yardstick of their times, and the paucity of their opportunities. They are milestones in the evolution of American art, for they set precedents that encouraged other Negro artists, and these in turn are still enriching our world. Without the courage and accomplishment of these pioneers, other black artists might never have attempted to overcome the handicaps of racial bias that compound the usual difficulties, economic and professional, faced by artists the world over.

American art, whether by white or black artists, developed slowly. In colonial days, all artistic effort had to be adjusted to the needs of a new land. The exigencies of pioneer life first had to be overcome in order to produce the leisure and wealth that is necessary before art can flourish. Also, strong cultural ties with mother countries existed for Europeans and Africans alike. We have already seen that the Negro artisan clung to his African culture as best he could. So, too, did the expatriate white colonist. It is therefore not surprising that the paintings hung in the earliest American homes were, like their owners, European in origin. Even after American artists began to develop in this country, most of them, both black and white, continued to obtain their training in Europe, where many established their reputations before they were accepted by the provincial colonists.

Nevertheless, there was slowly growing up in the colonies something that was neither African nor European but a quality we call "American." This trend began to make itself felt in various ways. Politically, the drive toward independence grew apace; informality replaced the frills and furbelows and protocal of the court-oriented societies of Europe, and alongside all this was an increasing respect for colonial workmanship. Local crafts and industries were developing, and American-made goods were becoming more desirable. It was not long before the European artists practicing in America began to receive considerable competition from native artists. Gradually, the spirit of America began to displace the European characteristics that had permeated art in this country.

Just what that spirit was would be hard to define. Certainly one quality was straightforward and direct reporting. The portraits by Copley, Stuart, and Morse, for instance, as well as those by such Negro artists as Joshua Johnston, convey an impression of unembroidered reality that follows the native tradition. The art critic, Peyton Boswell, has said, "An artist who capitalizes on the lessons of the Old World, and at the same time feels America as he paints her—to him we affix the label 'American'."

As more and more artists set up their own studios where others could be trained, American art began to develop its own distinct characteristics. Many important figures in the early days of American painting were self-taught, which may account for the variety and freshness of their work, unrestricted as they were by the hobbles of academicism. Many, like Gilbert Stuart (who eventually studied in England), received their early training in this country, either as pupils of some American artist or by watching other artists at work. Thomas Sully, for instance, commissioned Trumbull to paint a portrait merely in order to watch him, and Trumbull himself had, in turn, copied engravings and such paintings as he could find while still a student at Harvard. Art was not taught in schools until the mid-nineteenth century.

It was in this setting that we first distinguish one or two black artists by name. Whatever the African or European influences on them might have been, Negro artists in this country, like their white compatriots, tried to express a message of lasting interest that grew out of their American experience. It is because each artist's personal experience differed from the others' that their works have an individual character that is best understood and appreciated when we learn something of the varied lives of the artists themselves; for these, in turn, had a profound influence upon the direction their work was to take.

Until such patrons as the abolitionist groups and the Freedman's Bureau entered the picture in the nineteenth century, aspiring Negro artists had to depend on the enlightened attitudes of a few individuals. Even the talented free Negro was subject to all the legal restrictions, social opprobrium, and caprice of the slave system. To justify this system the European colonists had rationalized that by nature, temperament, pigmentation, and civilization—or lack of it—the Negro's natural lot was slavery and he was not fit for anything else. During colonial days the Negro artist was apt to be regarded as something of a curiosity; and since nineteenth-century provincialism tended to regard art as the ultimate expression of a civilized people, it was looked upon as a pretension for a Negro to identify himself with the creative arts.

Still, we occasionally catch a glimpse of a few Negroes of outstanding ability and drive who managed to become artists in spite of handicaps. Some, like Scipio Moorhead, we know of only through vague reports of their talents. Others, such as Joshua Johnston, have left their work as evidence but little of the man who produced it. They came from all walks of life and every part of the country, ranging from Moorhead, a lowly slave in New England, to Hudson, the elegant free mulatto in New Orleans. Well aware that only limited reports and records are available to us from a white-dominated world, we can only conjecture as to how many more there must have been whose works are unknown.

The following eighteenth-century advertisement from a Boston paper is typical of the scanty information one finds about the majority of Negro artists before the twentieth century:

Negro artist. At McLean's Watch-Maker, near Town-Hall, is a Negro man whose extraordinary Genius has been assisted by one of the best Masters in London; he takes faces at the lowest Rates. Specimens of his performance may be seen at said Place.

What was the name of this "extraordinary genius"? How did he manage to obtain an art education in London? What became of him? Where are his paintings now? Probably we will never know. He was an exceptional Negro, however, for few of his race had his advantage of study abroad. Most were either self-taught or had received limited instruction from some kindly patron. Much more typical is the slave mentioned in Peterson's *History of Rhode Island,* which states that Gilbert Stuart "derived his first impression of drawing from

*The Grocer's Children* by "Joe," an ex-slave; 1850s. (Courtesy, Milwaukee County Historical Society)

witnessing Neptune Thurston, a slave who was employed in his master's cooper shop, sketch likenesses on the heads of casks."

There are other tantalizing scraps of information that have come down to us, and by persistent effort more may yet be learned about such artists as G. W. Hobbs, a Methodist minister who resided in Baltimore around 1784. It is possible that he executed the pastel portrait of Richard Allen, first bishop of the African Methodist Church. We do know that Hobbs had virtually established himself as *the* portrait painter of the Methodist Episcopal Church in that area. Later, under the leadership of Bishop Daniel Payne, this church became a patron of the arts and did much to encourage talented young Negroes.

While the nineteenth century has left us far more documentation on Negro art than is available for the colonial period, it still leaves us with frustrating tangles and gaps. Much is known, for instance, about the life of Robert M. Douglass, Jr., yet his work has completely vanished. Vague or isolated references to Negro artists of the nineteenth century pique our curiosity. Portraits painted by two "colored mechanics" named Vidal and Wilson were exhibited in Philadelphia in 1852; they are mentioned in the New York *Herald* as being "very creditable." Three other Philadelphia artists matured about the same time as Douglass: William H. Dorsey, John P. Burr, and J. G. Chaplin; few examples of their work have survived. Similarly, the merits of Nelson Primus, A. B. Wilson, and Gerritt Loguen must remain unknown because either few or none of their works can be found. At least one Negro painter, Alexander Pickhil of New Orleans, destroyed nearly all his work in disgust over adverse criticism.

In fact, when one considers the difficulties of historical research, and the problem of identifying the work of artists who often left their pieces unsigned, it is really surprising that there are any authenticated examples of eighteenth- and nineteenth-century Afro-American art. Luckily this is not the case, and the artists themselves range from the distinguished Henry Ossawa Tanner, who was awarded the French Legion of Honor and was the first Negro to be elected a full member of the National Academy of Design in America, to untrained folk artists.

These "folk artists," or self-taught painters and sculptors, turned out work that is called "primitive" because of its lack of professional, academic technique. However, want of technical excellence in these artistic efforts is often more than compensated for by their fresh and original approach and the variety and interest of their subject matter. At Stratford Hall, in Virginia, there is a painting of a horse on one of the walls; according to tradition, it was done by a slave girl. No one knows her name, or the circumstances in which the picture was painted. And Harley, a slave in South Carolina, was moved to paint the battle of Fort Sumter; he also did a watercolor of the interior of the fort with its neat rows of quarters.

Two runaway slaves also turned their hands to painting. One, whose name we will never know, gratefully painted a small oil portrait of a banjo-player as a gift for the man who helped him escape. Joe, a runaway slave who was employed as a handyman and clerk in a grocery store in Milwaukee, Wisconsin, painted a portrait of the grocer's small daughter and son after his escape.

There may be countless more examples of work by Negro painters hanging unknown and unnoticed in private collections throughout the country. If only they could be recorded and made available for study by experts, many previously unidentified Negro artists might come to light.

J. Hall Pleasants produced enough clues to the identity of Joshua Johnston's work to uncover numbers of previously unknown examples of his art. Similarly, a painting by the nineteenth-century Negro artist, David Bustill Bowser, was recently identified from a photograph. This picture, even though it had been clearly signed and dated, had lain unnoticed in a National Park Service museum. Park Service officials valued it for its subject matter and knew nothing of Bowser except that he was a Negro.

One untapped source of Afro-American art may be the family portraits owned by American Negroes. Cedric Dover recognized that such paintings should be sought and studied. He believed them to be quite numerous and cited the Metoyer portraits at Melrose in Natchitoches, Mississippi, as examples worthy of further study. One is signed by Feuville, but whether he was a Frenchman or a Negro is not known. The other two are unsigned. A similar example is the interesting portrait of the distinguished Negro, William Whipper Boston businessman, editor, and writer, and the grandfather of actor Leigh Whipper. Done by an unknown artist, it is possibly the work of one of the group around William Matthew Prior of East Boston, but little investigation has been done to determine if any of these were Negroes. Painted at about the same period that William Simpson (discussed below) was working in Boston, its technique is much more primitive than Simpson's portraits of the Loguens, though it may be one of his early efforts. In any case, closer investigation might provide a solution to the mystery. Certainly such pictures invite further study.

Regardless of the outcome of such investigations, however, we already know of a number of pioneer Negro artists to whom Afro-Americans can point with pride.

*Mother and Daughter* by Joshua Johnston. (Courtesy, Museum of Early Southern Decorative Arts, Winston, Salem, N.C.)

## Scipio Moorhead (active around 1773)

One of America's earliest Negro artists was Scipio Moorhead, Boston slave. His memory has been preserved for us by the slave poet, Phillis Wheatley, who dedicated a poem "To S.M., a Young African Painter, on Seeing His Works." A penciled note in the 1773 edition of her volume, *Poems on Various Subjects, Religious and Moral,* identifies S.M. as "Scipio Moorhead, Negro servant to the Rev. John Moorhead of Boston whose genius inclined him that way."

None of this artist's work has ever come to light, but we are told that his talent was recognized and cultivated by Sarah Moorhead, wife of the minister, who was herself a teacher of art and expert in the techniques of drawing, japanning, and painting on glass. There is, unfortunately, no sound evidence that Scipio was the author of the unsigned portrait of Phillis Wheatley that is used as a frontispiece for several of her published works, but it affords interesting speculation. It is known that Phillis was acquainted with Scipio's owners and the conjecture that he made the portrait is strengthened when we realize that both the engraving and the poem to Scipio both appeared for the first time in the same 1773 edition of her work.

*Benjamin Franklin Joe and Son* by Joshua Johnston. (Courtesy, Museum of Early Southern Decorative Arts, Winston, Salem, N.C.)

## Joshua Johnston (active 1796–1824)

Although he is the best documented of all the eighteenth-century Negro artists, Joshua Johnston remains a shadowy figure at best. He was listed in the Baltimore Directory as a portrait painter, or limner, from 1796–1824, but following his death his works were often attributed to other artists. It has taken intensive research over the years to uncover some two dozen or so of his paintings.

Thanks to the efforts of the late Dr. J. Hall Pleasants of the Maryland Historical Society, we can draw a vague portrait of Joshua Johnston. That he was a "Free Householder of Colour" we know, and it appears likely that he was first a slave, or house servant, who later obtained his freedom, perhaps earning it through his labor as a painter. His work strongly suggests the direct influence of Charles Peale Polk, a relative of Charles Wilson Peale and a very active portrait painter in Baltimore in the 1790s. Tradition in the Moale family, whose portraits he painted, makes him the slave of Colonel John Moale, who lived on German Street in Baltimore, and at one time the artist is listed as residing no the same street, which seems to lend credence to this story. Perhaps he was given a studio on Colonel Moale's property.

Although Johnston moved frequently and lived at a succession of colorful addresses, such as Primrose Alley and Strawberry Lane, he must have been fairly successful when we consider the number of known paintings done by him for prominent Baltimore families. These indicate exceptional talent, especially when we realize that he must have been largely self-taught.

Johnston was a primitive painter, whose work has a two-dimensional quality, and his subjects are rendered in somewhat stiff and formal poses. But, the quaint simplicity of his style has a certain naïve charm; one cannot help but admire the obvious rapport that the artist established with his sitters.

In all of Johnston's portraits the poses are strikingly similar; the rather expressionless, pudgy hands are invariably holding some object. Since the same things appear and reappear in different pictures, they were probably props owned and used by the artist, rather than personal possessions of his sitters. In fact, two different members of the Bankson family are pictured wearing the same earrings! While sittings may have taken place in the artist's studio, it is possible the props were kept there and painted in without the sitter's presence, the faces being done separately at the subject's home. Such devices were frequently employed by limners to save the sitter's time. Because brass-studded Sheraton sofas and chairs are used frequently in Johnston's portraits, it has been conjectured that this "metallic rhythmic use of nails" is an Africanism. This seems very far-fetched, however. Had the actual nails themselves been inserted into the canvas there might be a clearer relationship; but since they are merely painted on, it is more likely these are, like the other artist's props, merely studio furnishings that were used because of their popularity at the time. Several other features make repeated appearances in Johnston paintings—baskets of strawberries or cherries; a letter, book, or map; the same large tassel; and a peculiar fuzzy white dog, with a piglike face, which may have been a pet of the artist.

### Robert M. Douglass, Jr. (1809–1887)

Born in Philadelphia in 1809, Robert M. Douglass, Jr. received a more than adequate Quaker education and attained recognition when he was only twenty-four. He was highly praised in *The Emancipator,* and Thomas Sully was impressed enough with his work to give Douglass "the highest commendations" in letters of introduction to friends in Europe. Numerous other letters and periodicals of the time prove that Douglass was a highly accomplished portrait and miniature painter. Among his known works are such varied pieces as a banner executed for the Grand Order of Odd Fellows in Philadelphia; a portrait of Fabré Geffard, President of the Republic of Haiti; drawings of missionary stations in Jamaica; and a lithographed likeness of William Lloyd Garrison, the abolitionist. Prints of the latter were placed on sale in New York City and Philadelphia for fifty cents each, and Douglass also mentioned that he had other portraits of distinguished philanthropists, all of which had been praised as "striking likeness." Yet not one of these numerous prints has come to light.

In letters written by the artist's sister, we learn that racial prejudice drove Douglass to emigrate in search of a more congenial environment, and that his application for a passport was rejected on the ground that "the people of color were not citizens and therefore he had no right to passports to foreign countries." It is not known how he finally managed it, but he did make two trips to the West Indies and eventually reached England. Frederick Douglass, then editor and publisher of *The North Star,* reprinted a letter from the artist sent from Jamaica, and comments that "he had gone there, in hopes the colors he uses, and the way he uses them, will be the tests of his merit, rather than that upon his own body, which he neither put on nor can rub off." Whether these hopes were realized we do not know, but the artist did return hopefully to the United States, as his advertising card in the *Pennsylvania Freeman* states:

Robert Douglass, Jr.
Portrait and Minature painter, No. 54 Arch St.
R.D. Jr. has studied drawing in the British Museum & at Saville House, Leicester Square and painting in the National Gallery in London . . . R.D. Jr. having acquired the above-mentioned arts by great labor and expense & having to struggle against peculiar difficulties, flatters himself that a liberal public will not refuse him encouragement.
Robert Douglass, Jr. died October 26, 1887, and remains a shadowy figure; his works are still undiscovered.

## Patrick Reason (1817–1850)

Patrick Reason, an artist-engraver, seems to have been sponsored principally as a propagandist for various antislavery organizations. His talent first became known when, at the age of thirteen, he designed the frontispiece for Charles C. Andrew's *History of the African Free Schools.* A few years later, through the efforts of New York abolitionists, Reason was apprenticed to a white engraver. And, later, as an independent draftsman and engraver himself, Reason did very creditable portraits of prominent men such as Governor De Witt Clinton of New York, the abolitionist Granville Sharp, and others, but he did not often turn his hand to figure composition. The most notable exceptions to this are Reason's copperplate engraving of the Certificate of Membership of the Masonic Fraternity and occasional frontispiece drawings such as the one that illustrates *Treadmill in Jamaica,* an autobiographical novel by James Williams, a slave.

The well-known antislavery symbol of a kneeling, suppliant slave, chains hanging from the wrists, is often erroneously attributed to Reason, but, in fact, though he did make an engraving of it, it is a copy. The original was designed by the famous William Hackwood, head modeler for Josiah Wedgwood, the English potter. It was ordered by Wedgwood in 1787 as a symbol for the British Anti-Slavery Society, of which he was a leading member. The first version of this figure, with its legend, "Am I Not a Man and a Brother?" appeared on a tiny oval medallion of Wedgwood pottery. Slightly over an inch long, with a black figure on a white ground, it was worn as jewelry or used on snuff boxes. Millions of copies followed, ranging from larger ones of Wedgwood to heavy bronze medals to the copy engraved by Reason.

While this artist's work has technical limitations, his importance lies in the fact that he was able to preserve the features of leading abolitionists with whom he had contact.

*Henry Bibb* by Patrick Reason. (Schomburg Collection, New York Public Library)

Murals at Belmont by Robert S. Duncanson. (Courtesy, The Taft Museum, Cincinnati, Ohio)

*Self-Portrait* by Julien Hudson; about 1839. (Collection of the Louisiana State Museum)

### Robert S. Duncanson (1817–1872)

Robert S. Duncanson, a mulatto of Scots-Canadian descent, was born in New York State, educated in Canada, and lived in Cincinnati or Detroit between trips to Europe and Canada. During his early years in Cincinnati he undoubtedly encountered the usual difficulties of all youthful artists, but he had the good fortune to be sent to Edinburgh, Scotland, to study at the expense of the Anti-Slavery League. There, as Dover says, paternal tradition led him to become "immoderately drunk on Tennyson and Scott." This resulted in a picture, based on Tennyson's poem, *The Lotus Eaters,* which received great acclaim from British art critics, though all attempts to locate it have failed.

This first trip abroad was followed by several others, including study of the "classical tradition" in Italy. Throughout Duncanson's sojourns abroad, however, he remained essentially an American artist, both in his work and his attitudes. Although he returned several times to Europe, he always came back to America, where he died.

During his residence in this country, Duncanson received numerous commissions to paint the portraits of prominent people of the day, including William and Freeman Cary, Bishop Payne, and the Berthelets. He did a full-length portrait of Nicholas Longworth, who commissioned him to execute a series of murals for the hall and reception room at Belmont, the Longworth mansion (now the Taft Museum) in Cincinnati.

A series of rather sentimental genre pictures punctuated his career as a landscape painter, which reached distinction in *Blue Hole, Flood Waters, Little Miami River,* a painting reminiscent of landscapes of the Hudson River School, which date from the same period. Though the charm of this picture was never quite repeated, he did produce several other lovely landscapes in the same romantic mood, including *Ellen's Isle, Loch Katrine, Vale of Kashmir,* and *Romantic Landscape.*

Present-day critics disagree in evaluating both Duncanson's artistic ability and his character as a person, but there is no doubt that Duncanson's career is a milestone in the history of Afro-American art, for he was perhaps the first American Negro artist to receive widespread recognition both at home and abroad.

### Julien Hudson (Active 1830–1840)

Little is known of Julien Hudson, a remarkable New Orleans artist, except that he was a teacher who studied in New Orleans and briefly, around 1837, in Paris. He was known for his miniatures and portraits; one of these is a self-portrait that supports the view that Hudson was an octoroon. It also reveals him as an extremely urbane young man, if not something of a dandy, with an interesting face. Both this and his portrait of Colonel Jean Michel Fortier, Jr., the commander of a corps of free Negroes at the Battle of New Orleans in 1815, prove his gift for portraying the character of his subjects.

### Eugene Warbourg (1825–1861)

Another Negro artist from New Orleans, Eugene Warbourg was a stonemason who shared a workshop with his brother Daniel. But while nothing of Daniel's work has come to light except graveyard memorials, Eugene chiseled a sufficient number of portrait busts and other sculpture for some to have survived. Desdunes, an obscure Creole teacher and writer from New Orleans, mentions that Warbourg was passionately devoted to art, and two of his works are remembered by name, *Le Pêcheur (The Fisherman)* and *Le Premier Baiser (The First Kiss).*

*Colonel Jean Michel Fortier, Jr.* by Julien Hudson;
about 1840. (Collection of the Louisiana State Museum)

*John Young Mason* by Eugene Warbourg. (Courtesy, Virginia Historical Society)

*Bishop Jermain Wesley Loguen* by William Simpson; about 1854. (Permanent Collection, Howard University Gallery of Art)

Cartoon by Henry Lewis, showing Uncle Sam watching Germany, Great Britain, and Russia pulling the world. (Courtesy, Margaret Burroughs, The DuSable Museum of African American History)

According to Desdunes, Eugene had a "natural penchant" for sculpture and received his first formal training under a French artist named Gabriel. When he began work as a professional artist, many notables sat for him, and he had no difficulty in obtaining commissions. The jealousy of other artists drove the sculptor to Paris, and to Rome, where he died. It was probably in Paris that he did the portrait bust, in neoclassical style, of John Young Mason, American minister to France in 1853. We are told that Warbourg represented Louisiana at the Paris Exposition of 1867.

### William Simpson (1818–1872)

We first learn of William Simpson from William Wells Brown, an early Negro writer and contemporary of Simpson. According to his reports, Simpson was a very productive portrait painter who also made "a sketch that hung in his studio, an allegory of summer which exhibited marked ability." As a youth, Simpson was punished for drawing in class instead of attending to his lessons, and he apparently began his career as the apprentice of "Mathew Wilson, Esq., the distinguished artist," in 1854. Later, as an independent artist, he drew patrons from several northern states as well as Canada, and his name is listed in the Boston Directories for 1860 and 1866. His portraits of the Loguens show both technical skill and a talent for portraiture.

### Henry Lewis (died 1890)

Henry Lewis is surely one of the earliest cartoonists of African ancestry. A clever artist, his satires were biting social commentaries on current events. Many of his cartoons pointed up the inequalities suffered by the Negro in the latter half of the nineteenth century. His work appeared in *Judge, Puck,* and other widely circulated magazines of the era, as well as in the *Indianapolis Freeman,* the first illustrated Negro newspaper in the United States.

### David Bustill Bowser (1820–1900)

Little is known of David Bustill Bowser's early life except that he was a cousin and pupil of Robert Douglass, Jr. His grandfather had been one of the first Negro schoolteachers in Pennsylvania, and it was in Philadelphia that Bowser supported himself as a painter of emblems and banners for fire companies and fraternal organizations. As far as his portraits and landscapes are concerned, he was strictly an occasional painter. Yet these works have survived the artist, while the only remaining example of his commercial work is an interesting insignia, inherited by one of his children, which he designed for the "Old Hose House" in Philadelphia.

Bowser received praise from the New York *Herald* on April 16, 1852: "The Marine Paintings of Bowser are excellent." The artist did a number of portraits of Abraham Lincoln, and relatives claim at least one of these was made from life, since a check made out in Lincoln's handwriting to David B. Bowser is still owned by Bowser's descendants (it was never cashed). A previously overlooked portrait of John Brown was uncovered by the author and is here reproduced for the first time.

### Edward Mitchell Bannister (1828–1901)

Born in Nova Scotia, Edward Mitchell Bannister was the son of a West Indian and a native of St. Andrews, New Brunswick. As a young man he is said to have shipped on a coastal steamer: this may have given him his love of the sea, which led to his settling first in Boston and later in Providence, Rhode Island, where he spent much of his time sailing on Narragansett Bay and in Newport Harbor.

Unlike most nineteenth-century Afro-American artists, Bannister enjoyed an excellent art education without ever going abroad. At Lowell Institute in Boston, he studied under the noted anatomist, Dr. William Rimmer, and throughout his life he enjoyed stimulating and helpful association with other artists. However, he remained an individualist. John Nelson Arnold, a fellow-artist and personal friend, mentions that in 1885 Bannister attended evening drawing classes at Lowell Institute. There a dozen or so artists drew from live models, and Arnold says of Bannister at this time that "from the first he followed no master nor any school, nothing but his own instincts."

Bannister first supported himself in Boston by making solar prints, which sold well and gave him the necessary leisure to sketch and paint scenes throughout the city. It was not long before he opened a studio and installed himself as a professional artist. His first commissioned work was *The Ship Outward Bound,* painted in 1854.

It is thought that as late as the end of the Civil War Bannister was uncertain of his commitment to painting as a profession and that perhaps the War itself, with the mighty issues it brought into focus, as well as his wife's activities on behalf of Negro troops, may have been the factors that decided him in that career. However, there are scarcely any social overtones in his paintings that indicate a particular awareness of the Negro situation in America.

In any case, it was not until the 1870s that he first received more than local recognition for his work. He was awarded a bronze medal, one of the first prizes, at the Philadelphia Centennial of 1876 for his painting *Under the Oaks.* This picture then sold for $1,500, a considerable sum for those days; unfortunately, the painting subsequently disappeared.

Both the Rhode Island School of Design and the Providence Art Club trace their origins back to the impact of this centennial. The huge display awakened visitors from across the country, giving them an awareness of the artistic gaps in their own communities. It was the impetus of the Centennial itself and of Bannister's recognition there that led the artist and two friends, Charles Walter Stetson and George W. Whitaker, to hold several informal meetings in Bannister's studio in Providence. Invitations were soon issued to other artists, which resulted in the formation of the Providence Art Club in 1878.

It has been said that this group became the nucleus of the Rhode Island School of Design, but the school was formed earlier and founded quite separately, although there is no doubt that both evolved from the same general impetus and that the young School of Design was fertilized by the Art Club. In the Memorial Exhibition for Bannister, held by the Art Club five months after the artist's death, we find among the owners of his paintings many names that are subsequently associated with the Museum of Art at the Rhode Island School of Design.

Although Bannister worked for years on a large canvas of *Christ in the Garden of Gethsemane,* it is for his New England landscapes that he is remembered best. In the latter part of the eighteenth century, Jean-Jacques Rousseau had sounded the call of "back to nature," and, in the reaction against the ugliness of the Industrial Revolution, the back-to-nature idea took root and became one of the more popular nineteenth-century escape mechanisms. So it was natural that Banninster, who loved the sea and the outdoors, settled on these as his subjects.

Most of Bannister's landscapes are bucolic, and he avoided the overt intrusion of grandeur into his pictures that was popular in the Hudson River School, which glorified and romanticized nature. Although Bannister obviously enjoyed the picturesque, he did not look at nature merely as a pleasing setting

*Portrait of John Brown* (detail) by David Bustill Bowser. Signed and dated 1858. (Collection of Harper's Ferry National Historical Park, W. Va. Courtesy, National Park Service)

*Lady with Bouquet* by Edward Mitchell Bannister. (Courtesy, Providence Art Club)

for idyllic scenes. Rather, he strove to paint what he saw, so the picturesque quality of his work is not contrived, but natural.

Bannister's continual study of skies and clouds during his sailing days enabled him to capture the changing moods of weather, especially the moments he liked most to depict—twilight, coming storm, or the aftermath of a storm—which imbued his landscapes with a mysterious, uncertain light and created an impression of grave tranquility.

*Landscape* by Edward Mitchell Bannister. (Courtesy, Providence Art Club)

### Edmonia Lewis (1845–1900?)

Of all the nineteenth-century Negro artists, the most intriguing character is Mary Edmonia Lewis. Edmonia, as she called herself in her later years, was an unusually talented and exotic woman, half American Indian, half Negro. Her Indian name was *Wildfire,* which expresses well her exuberant personality.

Born near Albany, New York, she was raised in the tribal life of her Chippewa mother, and probably thought of herself as Indian, rather than Negro. Her childhood was spent in typical Indian fashion, swimming, fishing, moccasin-making, and wandering in the wilderness, with occasional schooling in a white man's world. Orphaned while still a young girl, she entered Oberlin College, in Ohio, with the help of a brother.

Because of her Indian upbringing, it had been thought that she was too wild and undisciplined for formal study, but she apparently settled down and for three years followed the prescribed literary course. Her open and cheerful manner helped her to make friends easily, but led to a scandal that put an end to her college career. She was accused of poisoning two of her closest white coed friends. Although the judge at her hearing discharged her without trail, she left Oberlin under a cloud, amid vicious innuendoes that she was in fact guilty. Despite these crushing circumstances, Edmonia's spirit was not apparently damaged. Although she briefly considered leaving white society for good and returning to the Indian life of her childhood, fortunately she left her Oberlin experience behind and pursued a new career as an artist. With the help and encouragement of a Boston sculptor named Edmund Bracket, she soon opened her own studio with eight dollars donated by a "kindly lady." Edmonia then earned enough to study in Europe with proceeds from the sale of some one hundred copies that had been made from a bust she modeled of the Civil War hero, Colonel Robert Gould Shaw.

In Rome, with the help of William Wetmore Story (then doge of the New England expatriates there), the young Edmonia, not yet twenty, soon found a teacher and friend in Harriet Hosmer, the sculptress. In the unconventional art world of Italy, her eccentricities were accepted, and she was a sensation. There she found a cultural environment to encourage her bent for sculpture, and the artistic inspiration of the classical heritage.

William Fleming, in *Art and Ideas,* has remarked that "the cry of intellectuals at that period was 'Anytime but now and any place but here,' provided of course that this only applied to the books they read, the pictures they saw, and the music they heard." Edmonia benefitted from this reaction to the Industrial Revolution; the same one that accounted for the pastoral landscapes of Bannister and the romanticized wilderness scenes of Duncanson. Palm-fringed foreign shores, Oriental harems, and neoclassical sculpture had captured the popular imagination as a highly productive factory never could. In this market, Edmonia could not fail.

Edmonia has been described as attractive; she was radiant with self-confidence and a determination to utilize her art in the service of the "great struggle for freedom." As she said, "Mr. Garrison has given his whole life for

*Hagar* by Edmonia Lewis. (Frederick Douglass Institute of Negro Arts and History, Washington, D.C.)

my father's people and I think that I should give him a few months' work."

Passionate themes from American Indian folklore and Negro history followed closely on one another, and Edmonia's personality and shadowy personal history, as much as her talent as a sculptress, made her a celebrated and popular figure in art circles on both sides of the Atlantic. She was represented at the Philadelphia Centennial of 1876 by numerous works, a considerable recognition for a woman then barely thirty-one years of age, and especially remarkable for a Negro.

The Greek Revival was on the wane, however, and Edmonia's brief vogue was near its end; she sank into obscurity and finally oblivion. We do not even know the exact date of her death.

Among her best-known works are *Forever Free, Old Indian Arrow Maker and His Daughter,* and a series on Hiawatha, most of which have either disappeared or been destroyed. Two other pieces that were highly praised at the time of their execution but have since disappeared are *Freed-woman* and *Death of Cleopatra. Hagar,* biblically symbolic of the struggles of the Negro people, has recently reappeared. Some cherubic little children and several portrait busts also remain as examples of her talent.

### Annie Walker (1855–1929)

Little is known of Annie Walker except that she was born in Alabama and later went to New York City, where she studied at Cooper Union for the Advancement of Science and Art, the free school founded by Peter Cooper. Cooper Union enjoyed a fine reputation, then as now, and after graduation Annie moved to Paris, where she studied at the Académie Julien and exhibited in the Paris Salon of 1896. Only a few paintings remain to show us the sensitive character portrayal this young woman achieved.

### Meta Warrick Fuller (1859–1937)

Meta Warrick Fuller was one of those artists born in the 1800s whose career spanned the turn of the century. She studied first in Philadelphia, her hometown, but soon went to Paris, the mecca of all artists at that time. There, at the Académie Colarossi, she was a pupil of Rodin, who thought her promising.

Until 1910, when a fire destroyed most of her works, she was known as a "sculptor of horrors" because of the morbid character of her art. From that period on, however, her sculpture seems to have mellowed and to have become more expressive of her very charming personality.

### Henry Ossawa Tanner (1859–1937)

Henry Ossawa Tanner told of his early interest in painting. At the age of thirteen, while walking in Fairmount Park, Philadelphia, with his father, he was fascinated by the sight of an artist at work. This made such an impression on the boy that he hurried home and attempted to depict the same landscape from memory, using house-painter's brushes on the cardboard back of an old geography book.

Having chosen his career, Tanner pursued it with such increasing skill and application that even the opposition of his family could not deter him. His father, Bishop Benjamin Tucker Tanner of the African Methodist Episcopal Church, gave him all the support possible, once it was clear the boy's interest was genuine. For several years, Tanner worked hard at developing his technique, modeling the animals in the zoo in Philadelphia, painting seascapes, and studying under William Case and Thomas Eakins at the Pennsyl-

*La Parisienne* by Annie Walker; about 1896. (Permanent Collection, Howard University Gallery of Art)

*Waterboy* by Meta Warrick Fuller. (Harmon Collection in the National Archives)

*The Sabot Makers* by Henry Ossawa Tanner. A Breton scene reminiscent of other Negro genre paintings by Tanner. (Harmon Collection in the National Archives)

*Christ and His Mother Reading the Scriptures* by Henry Ossawa Tanner. (Harmon Collection in the National Archives)

vania Academy of Fine Arts, where he received a sound grounding in draftsmanship and painting techniques.

Eakins, who was a friend as well as a teacher, held that: "If America is to produce great painters and if young art students wish to assume a place in the history of the art of their country, their first desire should be to remain in America, to peer deeper into the heart of American life." This was heretical preaching, since at that time it was considered essential to study and work in Europe, which in the prevailing view was the fountainhead of all great art.

Unfortunately, Tanner failed to heed Eakins's advice, although for a time he taught at Clark University in Atlanta and spent his spare time painting landscapes and the folk of the North Carolina mountains. His work of this period, of which *The Banjo Lesson* is an example, hinted that at last Negro life would inspire a genre painter who could portray the Negro with sensitivity and understanding, but unfortunately this promise was not to be fulfilled.

At Clark University, Tanner was extremely unhappy, despite the encouragement and patronage of friends and admirers, notably Bishop Daniel A. Payne —who had helped many other Negro art students—and Bishop and Mrs. Joseph C. Hartzell. No doubt he experienced the usual race prejudice, and perhaps also mistook the obstacles faced by young artists the world over as further evidence of such discrimination, but in any case he became convinced he could not succeed in America and became determined to study abroad. Through the help of Bishop Hartzell, who arranged a one-man show for him and then ended up purchasing most of his paintings, Tanner finally succeeded in reaching Paris. Here he studied under Benjamin Constant and Jean-Paul Laurens at the Académie Julien.

At the Académie, Tanner developed a mature style grounded on his earlier work with Eakins and his admiration for Rembrandt, and he tried his hand at a variety of subjects. During summers in Brittany he painted a number of landscapes, including *Bois d'Amour, Evening Near Pont-Aven, Rocks at Concarneau,* and *Return of the Fishing Boats.* He also applied himself to a series of genre paintings of Breton life, which are reminiscent of his earlier pictures of Negroes in North Carolina. Such paintings as *The Bagpipe Lesson* and *The Sabot Makers,* which won favorable comment in the Paris Salon, show the same sensitivity for his subjects that we find in *The Banjo Lesson,* as well as a skillful interpretation of the play of light.

Originally destined for the ministry, and influenced by his father, Bishop Tanner, the artist had deep religious feelings that were expressed in his work. In the Paris Salon of 1896 he received honorable mention for a painting called *Daniel in the Lion's Den;* with the patronage of Rodman Wanamaker, Tanner went to Palestine, a trip that inspired a great biblical series that brought him fame. His success with this theme was followed in quick succession by others in the same sentimental vein. His paintings took prizes in the Paris Salons and were purchased by many of the leading American museums, including the Metropolitan Museum of Art in New York, Chicago Art Institute, and the Pennsylvania Academy of Fine Arts. The French Government made him a member of the Legion of Honor. In addition, he was the recipient of a gold medal from the Exposition Universelle Internationale and a bronze medal from the Panama-Pacific International Exposition. Most important of all, he became the first Afro-American to be elected a full member of the National Academy of Design.

In spite of this recognition of his considerable talent, Tanner remained an expatriate for forty-six years. Embittered by sensational publicity about his race, he became more and more a studio recluse. Out of contact with people, for whom he had such obvious empathy, his work became dry and academic.

Tanner's reputation was made on the basis of his vibrant "Tanner blues," striking subtleties of light, and clever use of tempera and oil in combination. Among his best-known paintings are *The Resurrection of Lazarus, The Disciples at the Tomb, Christ Walking on the Water, The Annunciation,* and *Christ and Nicodemus;* however, the recent discovery of some one hundred and fifty drawings, lithographs, etchings, and watercolors, which lay unnoticed for almost forty years in Tanner's dusty old studio in Paris, reveal a new dimension in his work. Many of these works are preliminary studies or sketches for his paintings, but in them the feeling and emotion of the artist are given spontaneous expression. No matter what the final evaluation of Tanner's art, the honors accumulated by him in his lifetime place him in a unique position in Afro-American art history.

Crayon study for *Peter* by Henry Ossawa Tanner. (Courtesy, Grand Central Art Galleries, Inc.)

# 7  RENAISSANCE AND DEPRESSION

*Mask, Lillian* by James Latimer Allen. (Photograph.)
(Harmon Collection in the National Archives)

*When the Tide is Out* by William Edouard Scott. (Harmon Collection in the National Archives. Photo, James L. Allen)

*French Scene* by Lois Mailou Jones. (Harmon Collection in the National Archives)

For generations the Negro artist in the United States followed the mainstream of American art, whether it was Greek Revival, romanticism, or academic realism, and during the nineteenth century, like other American artists, he looked to Europe for guidance. But soon after the turn of the century came a revolution in American art that the Negroes did not at first embrace.

America was fresh from a victorious war with Spain and embarking on a course of imperial expansion that later saw her assume the status of a world power. All this fostered national pride and a desire for independence from European influences. It was in part this impetus that gave birth to the Ashcan School, as it was derogatorily called, begun by eight "men of rebellion" who preached realism and believed that art should spring from everyday life. These white artists were rebelling principally against the currently popular academic pictures: pretty allegories, decorous virgins, pseudoclassical masquerades of grandeur, and other slavish copies of Paris Salon favorites. They believed that the artist must paint the life he knows best if he would be an American. This same viewpoint, of course, had been voiced earlier by Eakins, but few had listened; now artists were more receptive.

For the most part, these rebels' unorthodoxy lay only in their subject matter, but they prepared the way for the inquiring liberal spirit that made the modern movement the logical next step, and they were largely responsible for the now-famous Armory Show of 1913, which hit America like a bombshell and ushered in a new age of art.

World War I strengthened this iconoclastic movement, for, just as the American Revolution had done, it accelerated a patriotic "Paint American" and "Buy American" movement; Americans suddenly came back to reality in the grip of adversity and once again began to rely on their own resources.

But the ferment caused by these events made little impact on the work of Negro artists, who remained aloof for some time from the various cliques of white artists, which were forming and re-forming in the art world.

The tremendous impact of Henry Tanner's success probably accounted for this conservatism and the Negroes' obvious preference for academic realism and a modified impressionistic style. They continued to travel and study abroad when possible; Meta Warrick Fuller has already been mentioned, and there were others, as well, who studied or worked in Europe. Both William Harper and William Edouard Scott were pupils of Tanner, and Lois Mailou Jones studied at the Académie Julien. Hale Woodruff, Aaron Douglas, Palmer Hayden, Archibald Motley, James A. Porter, and Elizabeth Prophet are also among those who went abroad during this period; some, like William H. Johnson and Alexander Smith, became expatriates for a number of years.

These world travelers turned out some interesting interpretations of the foreign scene, and the exhibitions of this period abound in landscapes and genre subjects from France, Scandinavia, Italy, North Africa, and the Caribbean. Even in these more traditional subjects, a growing individuality of expression can be seen in the variety of styles and techniques. According to James A. Porter, the paintings of Lois M. Jones were "in the tradition, but not in imitation, of Cezanne," and what Hale Woodruff learned from the Europeans "has been minted in color and brilliant muscular composition." William Johnson, a native of Florence, South Carolina, went through a sophisticated development from academicism to expressionism before developing the intentionally naïve style of his later work.

Meanwhile, the migration of Negroes from the rural South into the urban

North during World War I had brought great concentrations of them into contact with the cultural and educational opportunities of large cities, especially New York, which had begun to rival Paris as a mecca for American artists, writers, actors, and musicians. This made its impression on the migrants, and by the 1920s a cultural rejuvenation of Negroes was under way, not only in Harlem, but in Washington and Chicago as well. The seeds of this Negro Renaissance had begun earlier, however. In 1903, W. E. B. DuBois had written *The Souls of Black Folk* and had voiced the feelings of Negroes within the framework of a white society. Until that time, black people had generally considered their own yearnings, beliefs, and attitudes as matters of purely personal concern. In *The Souls of Black Folk,* they discovered a bond of common grievances and a language through which to express them. All this was to have a profound effect on the Afro-American artist.

Negro intellectuals strove to give direction to the welter of cultural exchange and social assimilation that was taking place, but until 1925 there was little assistance for the painters and sculptors striving to find their niche within this Negro Renaissance. It was in that year that the Negro scholar-aesthete, Dr. Alain Leroy Locke, wrote *The New Negro,* which epitomized, and gave a name to, the ferment of artistic and literary endeavor among Negroes. This book was the first to present a number of paintings and drawings representative of the new trends in Negro art.

One of these trends was an inclination toward racialism in painting and sculpture. This viewpoint was nurtured and interpreted by Dr. Locke, who became the principal spokesman of the Negro Renaissance. Sir James Frazer's anthropological work, *The Golden Bough,* had brought about an interest in primitive art, which first influenced such European modernists as Picasso and Modigliani and then reached America. Keenly aware of this, Locke amassed a considerable collection of African sculpture himself and urged strongly that all significant art has its roots deep in the soil that produced the artist. He insisted that Negro artists must link their present with their past. Many resisted his counsel, but his thesis did have its effect on the work of several artists in the New Negro Movement.

Such internal counsel for racial self-expression, and the external pressures of American realism (which were at last being felt), raised the basic issue of racial representation in and through art. For a while it divided the artists into two camps—those who followed the mainstream of realism and those who felt the need for some sort of racial expression. Torn between a practical need to meet the commercial requirements of publishers, or acceptance by the white-dominated buying public, and their newly found sense of racial identity, a few Negro artists developed split artistic personalities as they oscillated between the two viewpoints.

By the mid-twenties, a combination of realism, Americanism, and cultural racialism won dominance in what was the first group-conscious school of Afro-American art. A few of the traditionalists, such as May Howard Jackson, Archibald Motley, and Laura Wheeler Waring, aligned themselves with this group and were joined by such pioneering talents as Aaron Douglas, Sargent Johnson, Richmond Barthé, Palmer Hayden, William H. Johnson, Hale Woodruff, Malvin Gray Johnson, and others.

A most important tenet of the new creed was an avowed acceptance of racial self-portraiture and self-expression as the primary goal of the Negro artist. Previously, most Afro-American artists had assiduously avoided racial subjects for fear of being labeled "Negro artists"; this, they feared, would prevent impartial judgment of their work. The New Negro Movement broke

*Frankie* by Laura Wheeler Waring. (Harmon Collection in the National Archives)

*Anna Washington Derry* by Laura Wheeler Waring. (National Collection of Fine Arts, Smithsonian Institution)

111

*Self-Portrait* by Rex Goreleigh. (Harmon Collection in the National Archives)

*My Mother* by James A. Porter. (Harmon Collection in the National Archives)

*Woman Holding a Jug* by James A. Porter. (Harmon Collection in the National Archives)

*Portrait of the Artist's Wife* by Edwin A. Harleston. (Harmon Collection in the National Archives)

the limiting stereotypes through which the Negro and Negro life traditionally had been seen. By freeing the black artist from avoidance of such subject matter, it eventually led him to more objective and effective self-portrayal. The new feeling of racial identity and pride erupted in a growing number of artistic works in the Negro idiom. Some striking pictures of Negro life and character were the result. Both Laura Wheeler Waring and Edwin A. Harleston of the older generation had already been devoting their talents to Negro portraiture and continued to do so during this period. They were now joined by many younger artists, such as James A. Porter, Malvin Gray Johnson, Hale Woodruff, Lois Mailou Jones, Archibald Motley, and William Johnson. John Wesley Hardrick, William Edouard Scott, Robert Savon Pious, and Albert Alexander Smith also authored several fine character studies of Negro types. James Latimer Allen was one of the few artists to adopt photography as his medium. His creative portrait studies of black people are outstanding.

Some painters and sculptors took the advice of the racial apologists quite literally, and they began to look to the ancestral arts of Africa for inspiration. Outstanding among these were the painters Aaron Douglas, Hale Woodruff, and James L. Wells, as well as the sculptors Richmond Barthé and Sargent Johnson. These men all disclose in their work a conscious attempt to find expression for their African roots and a growing familiarity with African art forms. Unfortunately, most Afro-American artists were without a clear conception of the principles that underlie this great art. Imitating in self-conscious fashion their naïve impressions of African sculpture, many of their early paintings and sculpture illustrate their weakness. A few merely gave token homage to this theme, as did Malvin Gray Johnson, in his *Self-Portrait,* and Palmer Hayden in *Fetiche et Fleurs.*

Aaron Douglas is sometimes spoken of as the first exponent of the "New Negro," and his unique illustrations for James Weldon Johnson's *God's Trombones* were followed by his equally original murals for Fisk University and for the 135th Street Library in New York City, now the home of the Schomburg Collection of the New York Public Library. Critics disagree, however, when it comes to seeking "Africanisms" in these works. One can find just a faint hint of Africa in their symbolic character and the rhythmic, decorative patterns. But the broken, overlapping planes and the abrupt changes of line and mass are more closely related to Cubism, which obtained its inspiration directly from Africa. Certainly Douglas's murals are original and satisfying. They reflect the innovative spirit of the Modernists and mark a turning point for the Negro artist. From that moment on, the use of symbolic rather than purely representational forms was evident in much of Afro-American art. Most of Douglas's murals are based on themes from Negro history. They were the forerunners of others to follow by Charles Alston, Vertis Hayes, Hale Woodruff, Charles White, John Biggers, Carroll Simms, Jack Jordan, and many others.

In the 1920s, the question of how and what to paint plagued the Negro even more than his white fellow-artist. No matter what subjects he selected, he was still criticized as an imitator. The critics were accustomed to thinking of Negroes in terms of their differences rather than their similarities to other Americans, and unless they were portrayed as stereotyped caricatures, or in exotic or picturesque settings, they were at best considered dull and uninteresting, and at worst imitative of white America.

*Blind Sister Mary* by William Edouard Scott. (Harmon Collection in the National Archives)

*Self-Portrait* by William H. Johnson. (Harmon Collection in the National Archives)

*Fetiche et Fleurs* by Palmer Hayden. This rare still life of Hayden's reflects a naïve response to Locke's plea to "return to the ancestral arts," with its mislabeled "Fetish." (Harmon Collection in the National Archives)

*George Washington Carver by* Richmond Barthé. (Harmon Collection in the National Archives)

*African Fantasy* by James Lesesne Wells. (Harmon Collection in the National Archives)

*Copper Mask* by Sargent Jonnson. (Harmon Collection in the National Archives)

*African Dancer* by Richmond Barthé. (Collection of Whitney Museum of American Art, New York. Photo, Geoffrey Clements)

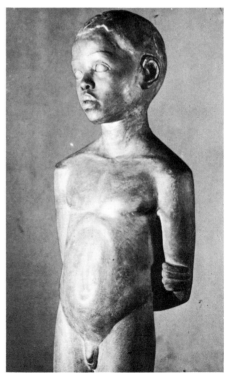

*Anderson* by Sargent Johnson. (Harmon Collection in the National Archives)

Fortunately, there were many who met this challenge courageously, encouraged by another spokesman for the New Negro, Langston Hughes, who said:

> We younger Negro artists who create now intend to express our individual dark-skinned selves without fear or shame. If white people are pleased we are glad. If they are not, it doesn't matter. We know we are beautiful. And ugly, too. If colored people are pleased we are glad. If they are not, their displeasure doesn't matter either. We build our temples for tomorrow, strong as we know how and we stand on the top of the mountain, free within ourselves.

This newly discovered freedom was most evident in the variety of styles and subjects adopted by the Negro artist at the time. Trying first one and then another of the various -isms that swirled through the art world at that time, the Negro artist was gradually finding himself. Cubism, expressionism, realism, constructivism, abstractionism, and regionalism are but a few of the almost infinite range of choices that confronted the twentieth-century artist. For the Negro artist, however, a multiplicity of styles rather than an overall unity seems to be characteristic. Although the twenties and thirties might best be described as a period of experimentation for the Negro, the liberating theories of the day helped him to escape from the timid conformity of previous generations.

In subject matter, as well as in styles and techniques, the Afro-American artist was becoming increasingly emancipated. As more and more artists listened to the voices of the New Negro Movement and became concerned with chronicling and interpreting their own lives and history, and the lives of their neighbors, foreign subjects gradually diminished. For the first time, most Afro-American artists were indeed heeding Eakin's advice to "peer deeper into American life." And so this increasing trend away from escapism —this coming to grips with reality—resulted in a fresh search for values and ideas in the immediate surroundings.

Some of the pictures that came from this search are timeless, like the vibrant pictures of Virginia rural life with which Malvin Gray Johnson crowned his career just before his untimely death in 1934. But Archibald Motley painted a period—the mad Roaring Twenties, the twenties of Harlem with its Cotton Club and its teeming city life of gin mills, streetwalkers, gamblers, and all the other inhabitants of that world. Others followed with scenes from dockyard and factory, tenant farm and city street. The artist's quest took him into the homes of the great and the humble; he explored Negro spirituals and folklore, as well as the history of his people.

In spite of these emancipating influences, however, the Negro artist still had to face one more handicap—the double standard of performance and judgment in the national picture.

To encourage striving young artists and writers, the Amy Spingarn prizes of 1924 were set up under the aegis of *The Crisis* magazine "for persons of Negro descent in order to encourage their aptitude for art expression." Those artists who had already been working without acclaim or criticism were singled out for recognition. The writers Langston Hughes and Countee Cullen and the artists Laura Wheeler Waring and Edwin A. Harleston were among the first winners of these awards.

Then came the exhibitions and awards sponsored by the Harmon Foundation between 1926 and 1933. It is almost impossible to appreciate fully the contributions made to the development of modern Negro art by this forum.

*Self-Portrait* by Malvin Gray Johnson. (Harmon Collection in the National Archives)

*Self-Portrait with Pipe* by William H. Johnson. (Harmon Collection in the National Archives)

Murals at 135th Street Library, New York City, by Aaron Douglas. (Harmon Collection in the National Archives)

Easel painting for Treasury Relief Art project by Archibald Motley. (Harmon Collection in the National Archives)

*Dixie Madonna* by Malvin Gray Johnson. One of six rural sketches, Brightwood, Va. (Harmon Collection in the National Archives)

Amistad Murals in the Savery Library, Talladega College, Ala., by Hale Woodruff. Painted in 1939, the the centennial of the Amistad incident. First panel: *The Mutiny.* (Harmon Collection in the National Archives)

*Checker Game* by William Hayden. (Harmon Collection in the National Archives)

*Formal* by Charles Alston. (Harmon Collection in the National Archives)

*Back Room—Gin Mill* by Charles Alston. (Harmon Collection in the National Archives)

*Jacobia Hotel, Florence, S. C.* by William H. Johnson. (Harmon Collection in the National Archives)

*Power Plant* by Aaron Douglas. (Harmon Collection in the National Archives)

*Old Death* by Henry Bozeman Jones. (Harmon Collection in the National Archives)

*There Were No Crops This Year* by Charles White. This charcoal drawing won a first award at the American Negro Exposition in Chicago in July, 1940. (Harmon Collection in the National Archives)

Certainly it was not faultless. Critics have said that the work selected by the juries "was not technically or subjectively homogenous," and that there was a conglomeration of styles. Even the artists themselves complained that the more mature and competent works were hung beside the naïve and inexperienced, that modernism was mixed with traditionalism. Romare Bearden, then a student, protested that it "encouraged the artist to exhibit long before he has mastered the technical equipment of his medium," and "it has allowed the Negro artist to accept standards that are both artificial and corrupt."

There was much truth in the accusations that the judges were too liberal in subject and had not enough concern for execution; that there was a certain ambivalence in the attitudes of the Harmon Foundation officials. They appeared to consider, on the one hand, that Afro-American artists should be judged without regard to race; on the other hand, it seemed at times as though their only criterion for artistic excellence was blackness of skin.

The objectives of these exhibits, stated in the catalog for the Harmon Foundation exhibit of 1933, were admirable: the encouragement of the Negro artist, the development of Negro art, and the promotion of the Negro theme and subject as a vital phase of the artistic expression of American life. Critics fail to realize that while patronizing the mediocre as well as the good, the Harmon Foundation was also sponsoring the future masters of Negro art, and that one of its most important services was to provide opportunities for Afro-American artists to receive criticism. The exhibitions helped focus both public and professional attention on the needs and the accomplishments of Negro artists. Never before had the race as a group been singled out for attention in this field, and, with the impetus provided by the Harmon Foundation exhibitions, Negro art developed a momentum of its own.

In just a short span of time, this was evident. In 1925, William E. Harmon, who had organized the Foundation as a social welfare experiment, decided to give recognition for outstanding creative work by American Negroes. No one knew how many artists there might be. Six or eight were mentioned as possibilities, but nineteen artists ventured to submit their work. From this small beginning, the number of exhibitors increased each year, so that in five years a total of 125 artists participated. A mere glance at the list of early award winners shows that from these have come some of the truly great names in modern Negro art: Palmer Hayden, Hale Woodruff, Laura Wheeler Waring, John W. Hardrick, Sargent Johnson, Archibald Motley, Jr., May Howard Jackson, Malvin Gray Johnson, William E. Artis, James Lesesne Wells, James Latimer Allen, and James A. Porter.

In fact, the list of Harmon Foundation exhibitors reads like a *Who's Who* of Afro-American art. Although many of the lesser artists found worthy oblivion, and others, like Malvin Gray Johnson, unfortunately died early, most of the consistent exhibitors and winners went on to greater achievement and recognition. America indeed owes a debt of gratitude to William Harmon and to the devotion of Mary Beattie Brady, the Harmon Foundation's dedicated director.

The Negro Renaissance was not to last. The Great Depression that followed so devastatingly on the heels of the Roaring Twenties effectively ended this exciting period. The warm feeling of kinship, the stimulating exchange of ideas, the increased pride of race and accomplishment that had burgeoned were overwhelmed in a flood of poverty and bankruptcy. Many of the Negro literary and art publications that came into being during the decade folded under the economic pressure, and many promising artists and writers failed to survive the crisis.

*Field Workers* by Ellis Wilson. (National Collection of Fine Arts, Smithsonian Institution)

*Resting* by Claude Clark. (National Collection of Fine Arts, Smithsonian Institution)

*Cabin Days* by Dox Thrash. Carborundum print, a graphic process invented and developed by Thrash. (Harmon Collection in the National Archives)

*Going to Church* by William H. Johnson. An example of the artist's style in the final period of his life, it is deliberately naïve and primitive. Johnson was a prolific painter: there are some 1,100 examples of his work in the National Collection of Fine Arts alone! (Harmon Collection in the National Archives)

"John Henry" series by Palmer Hayden. *Steam Driller and John Henry*. (Harmon Collection in the National Archives)

*Divine Love* by Sargent Johnson. (Harmon Collection in the National Archives)

*The Escape of the Spies from Canaan* by James Lesesne Wells. (Harmon Collection in the National Archives)

Yet, paradoxically enough, another avenue for the expansion of Negro creativity was actually opened up by the Depression. This period broadened the horizons of many Afro-American artists and provided an opportunity for developing their talents that would not have been available otherwise: thanks to Franklin D. Roosevelt's New Deal, the projects of the Federal Arts Programs both fed the body and nourished the talents of Negro artists, many of whom participated in the various Federal Arts Projects of the W.P.A. and the Treasury Department.

The Federal Arts Programs resulted in a significant contribution to American art. When inventory was taken on March 1, 1939, the Section of Fine Arts had purchased 539 murals and sculptures for the decoration of public buildings throughout the country. Many of these had been done by Negroes, notably Charles Alston, Vertis Hayes, Archibald Motley, Allan Crite, and Charles White.

One of the dividends of these programs was the opportunity for Negro artists to devote full time to their art. Theretofore, art had been for many an avocation, a part-time luxury, and talented artists like Richmond Barthé had been forced to support themselves by working as busboys, porters, butlers, or caretakers. The Federal programs both expanded the horizons of the older artists and helped to develop a younger generation of artistically ambitious Negroes. William Artis, Elizabeth Catlett, Eldzier Cortor, Fred Flemister, Jacob Lawrence, Ellis Wilson, Hughie Lee-Smith, and Charles White were some of the promising young painters and sculptors whose careers were advanced through the W.P.A.

Exhibitions of Negro art increased; both group and one-man shows were held, among them "The Hall of Negro Life," or the Federal Negro Building, as it was called, at the Texas Centennial Exposition in 1936; and Contemporary Negro Art, at the Baltimore Museum of Art in 1939. At the First American Artist's Congress in 1936, only one Negro among 360 was present, but even this token recognition was a step forward. The Whitney Museum's purchase of Elizabeth Prophet's *Congolaise* and several of Barthé's works in 1932 had been followed by increasing national recognition. Motley and Barthé, as well as Tanner, were represented at the Century of Progress in Chicago in 1933, and Augusta Savage was commissioned to execute a piece, for the New York World's Fair of 1939, which would "convey the spirit of American Negro music." This resulted in her striking, harplike sculpture, *Lift Every Voice*. Also, through the sponsorship of dealers like Robert Carlen and institutions like the Museum of Modern Art in New York City, previously unknown primitives, like Pippin and Edmondson, received prominence.

In the summer of 1940, the significant Exhibition of the Art of the American Negro was assembled by Alonzo Aden of Howard University, with the cooperation of the Harmon Foundation and the W.P.A., and held at The American Negro Exposition in Chicago. Two other noteworthy exhibits followed in close succession in 1941, one in the McMillen Galleries and another at the Downtown Gallery, both in New York. The latter was prolonged and eventually evolved into an exhibit organized in 1945 by John Davis Hatch for the Albany Institute of History and Art; it was called "The Negro Artist Comes of Age." For the catalog of this exhibition Alain Locke wrote an introductory essay entitled "Up Till Now." In it he said that the growing democracy in American art had "brought forward the common denominators of a truly representative native American art, which logically has included the serious interpretation of the Negro elements in the national whole. This democratically shared interest has brought the Negro artist into closer rapport and collaboration with his fellow American artists."

120

One of the most significant aspects of the thirties and forties was the increase of interest and participation in the arts by the Negro public. Under the combined stimuli of the Negro Renaissance, the Federal Arts Programs, and the activities of the Harmon Foundation, there developed a growing community of Negro patrons of the arts. Through the efforts of the Harmon Foundation, art education in Negro schools and colleges had expanded; in 1942, under the able leadership of Hale Woodruff, Atlanta University inaugurated an annual exhibition of the works of Negro artists. From each showing, selections made by juries were purchased by the University. Out of these Atlanta exhibitions was born the National Conference of Artists. Its purposes were expressed by Charles White, one of its members, when he said that he hoped the first Conference would "serve to inspire our artists to create works permeated with great ideas and great passions," as well as "inspire the Negro people to embrace our works with all their love."

In fact, the Negro people had already begun to "embrace their works with love," for even in the thirties the art workshops and community art centers produced more art than the colleges. Workshops, "thumb-tack galleries," salons, and art guilds were organized in theaters, churches, libraries, and schools, as the Harmon Foundation's *Review of Achievements* in 1935 shows. In Harlem, the interrelated activities of the Artists' Guild, the Art Center, the Art Workshop, and the Alston-Bannarn Studios were reinforced by the Savage Studio of Arts and Crafts, as well as the cultural programs emanating from the Countee Cullen branch of the New York Public Library, under the leadership of Arthur Schomburg, Curator of the Department of Negro Literature, History, and Prints.

Nor was this sort of activity restricted to Harlem. It spread from one end of the country to the other, and, although some of these organizations served the purpose of the moment and then died, others are still alive and functioning today. The South Side Community Art Center in Chicago, for instance, was set up by the W.P.A. Federal Arts Project for Illinois, but it is still a vital force and focal point for artists in the Chicago area. In Cleveland, Negro artists still have the support and facilities provided by Karamu House, whose programs were founded by Russell and Rowena Jelliffe in 1915. The Conference of Artists is still an active organization, and there are others too numerous to mention. These achievements were chronicled in James A. Porter's *Modern Negro Art,* published by Dryden Press. Indispensable to scholars and students alike, it is a milestone in itself, as the first Negro art history ever to be published.

*Crispus Attucks* by William H. Johnson. (Harmon Collection in the National Archives)

*John Brown Goes to His Hanging* by Horace Pippin. (Courtesy, Pennsylvania Academy of the Fine Arts)

*Mother and Child* by William Edmondson. (Courtesy, The Museum of American Folk Art, New York)

# 8 CONTEMPORARY NEGRO ART AND CRAFT

*Daybreak, A Time to Rest* by Jacob Lawrence. (Courtesy, Terry Dintenfass Gallery)

*Boy with Tire* by Hughie Lee-Smith. (Courtesy, The Detroit Institute of Arts)

*The Family* by Charles Alston. (Collection of Whitney Museum of American Art, New York)

It is always difficult to assess the present, because we are too close for objectivity. When we look into the past, certain things stand out, in spite of the confusing details of history—the service to god and king in Africa; the struggle toward acculturation in an alien society during the slavery period; the efforts of early Afro-American artists to mold themselves into a white image; and the growing feeling of racial identity and pride during the Negro Renaissance. It is a different matter when we come to the contemporary scene.

In 1945, Alain Locke, encouraged by recent progress, hopefully stated, "If the gains of the last five years are matched by the next five, by 1950 we shall have realized almost complete democracy in American art, which will be as significant and valuable an achievement for the national culture as for the Negro." Unfortunately, it is not possible to report that his wish came true. Yet there have been material gains toward this goal.

It is not within the scope of this book to analyze the contributions of Afro-Americans to contemporary art. The purpose of this concluding chapter is, rather, to mention some of the artists whose work has already been acknowledged important, to touch on some of the issues that concern black artists today, and to note some current trends whose outcome has yet to be seen and whose effects cannot yet be assessed.

Many of the names made familiar during the Negro Renaissance are still in the news. Some artists are concentrating on gallery work, while others have gone into teaching, acquiring advanced degrees and a reputation for excellence along the way. A few have combined two or more careers with success. Most of the art teachers continue to paint or sculpt; many with reputations as gallery artists also teach part time. In part because of their guidance and encouragement, new generations of black artists have entered the field. In fact, the number of Negroes in the arts has so multiplied that one can no longer list them, and it is practically impossible even to note the variety of fields into which they have ventured.

However, in spite of the fact that Negroes have joined an increasing number of art faculties and have gained recognition in other areas as well, they have generally not become part of what has been called "the cliquish art establishment." Yet Jacob Lawrence, Al Hollingsworth, Romare Bearden, and Hughie Lee-Smith are among several successful Afro-American artists whose names are widely known and whose work is handled by prestigious galleries, those professionally operated showrooms and sales galleries that act as middlemen between the artist and the purchaser. In New York, Terry Dintenfass, Grand Central, Cordier and Ekstrom, and Midtown Galleries all have featured black artists, both in groups and in one-man shows.

Perhaps the most striking feature of contemporary Negro art is its eclecticism, not only in the narrow sense of subject matter and techniques, or in the broader spectrum of its fields, but also in its philosophy. In discussing aesthetics or purpose, hardly any two black artists will express the same views.

The old question of the racial content of art still arises. Every now and then the artists stop and debate hotly among themselves whether their work should be applied directly to the activities of the Civil Rights Movement; whether they have special qualities to express as Negro artists; what their value is as artists who are both American and Negro; to what degree and in what manner successful Negro artists can use their success as a weapon or as a resource to improve the status of Negroes in society. But there seems to be no consensus of opinion. As during the New Negro Movement, there tends to be a certain amount of polarization; some artists go quietly about their work, abstaining from polemics and erudite discussions of aesthetics

A visionary and inspired painting by Minnie Evans, a
76-year-old folk artist. "Something told me to draw,
or die," she says.    (Collection  Old  Slave  Mart
Museum. Photo, author)

*Confrontation* by Merton Simpson. One of many versions of this picture painted by Simpson.

*Freedom Now* by Reginald Gammon; 1965. Acrylic on board.

or racial commitments; others verbalize loudly. Counterbalancing those who feel that art should be used to solve sociological and anthropological problems are others who believe just as strongly that it must be created, judged, and consumed largely in terms of its universal values.

Two interesting forums should be mentioned. In 1963, the Spiral Group, under the leadership of Hale Woodruff, Romare Bearden, and Charles Alston, discussed many questions raised by contemporary Negro artists. They attempted to analyze that certain *something* that they believed set them apart from other painters; they called it "the Negro Image." But it was difficult to discover whether this "Negro Image" is something tangible that can be transmitted through art, and, if so, just what it is. As before, the answers were disparate. Some followed the proponents of *négritude,* or "blackness," in believing that black people everywhere, regardless of nationality, possess something in common that is translated into their creative work of whatever nature—literature, drama, music, or applied art. In 1966, at the First World Festival of Negro Art, in Dakar, Senegal, this concept was discussed at an eight-day colloquium on "The Function and Meaning of African-Negro Art in the Life of the People," and it was hotly disputed. The results were inconclusive, but the arguments proved that many Africans, Europeans, and Americans consider the concept of *négritude* racist and regard it as an attempt to justify Pan-Africanism. Many black intellectuals and artists refused to be identified with it and boycotted the Festival.

Proponents of *négritude* or of the "Negro image" claim to see reflections of common emotional factors of racial life and experience in the work of Negro artists, or they see an unusual degree of strength and virtuosity of color and rhythm, as well as vivid originality of imagination. However, it is difficult to say how much of this interpretation is knowledge after the fact. If, for instance, one judges Negro art alongside that of artists of other ethnic origins, without knowing which is which, it is questionable whether anyone can perceive the color of the creative hand by even the most scrupulous examination of the artistic work. Many Negro artists believe such perception is neither possible nor preferable. They think it better to avoid judgment on the basis of race, for fear of partiality.

Over and above the entire problem of *intent,* or of obligation to racial objectives, however, there remains the question of *content,* the result after the work is completed. And, if the contemporary Negro artist is to be judged by what he does, rather than by what he says, one is forced to the conclusion that in most cases he aims at universality in his work. He does have something to offer that no other artist has, but only in the sense that regardless of his cultural, national, or ethnical origins, every artist is different from all others in terms of his human uniqueness. Each person paints out the life he lives, and the Negro artist and his ancestors can lay claims to unique racial experiences.

Much of contemporary Negro art may take on the superficial aspects of a racial art, but it possesses universal values, too. Thus, when Hughie Lee-Smith pictures a solitary Negro boy on a rooftop or playing with a tire in a drab city street, he is not only saying something about Negroes but about loneliness and isolation in general. Similarly, Al Hollingsworth's anguished *Cry City* is applicable to all city minorities, of whatever color. And certainly Ernie Crichlow's *White Fence* is both racial and universal in import.

The individuality that appears to be characteristic of the Negro artist in regard to racial commitment is also evident in his choice of subject matter, media, techniques, aesthetics, and fields. All are becoming increasingly diversified.

126

*Cry City* by Al Hollingsworth. Polymer, oils, and fluorescent oils, egg-crates, and charcoal on Masonite. (Courtesy of the artist)

*Harbor* by Al Hollingsworth. (Courtesy of the artist)

*The Library* by Jacob Lawrence. (Courtesy, National Collection of Fine Arts, Smithsonian Institution)

*Palm Sunday Procession* by Romare Bearden; 1967. Collage. (Cordier & Ekstrom Gallery, New York)

*Poultry Market* by Walter Williams. (Collection of Whitney Museum of American Art, New York)

Some artists, like Lee-Smith, having discovered their own unique means of expressing themselves, have remained with it. Their work is immediately recognizable. Jacob Lawrence has continued to paint in the narrative style that is so unmistakably his that his work needs no signature. Romare Bearden's cubist-surrealist collages are also executed in personal idiom that is totally unlike that of any other artist. Both Lawrence and Bearden have adopted Negro subject matter, but, as Romare Bearden says, this does not in itself make the work *Negro*. He points out that "There are certain experiences within the Negro life style that are similar to all the great and common experiences of art...."

Other Negroes are continually exploring new ideas, new techniques, and new media, and responding to the stimuli of current events. The resulting changes are sometimes so complete it is difficult to recognize the artist in his work. In the troubled days of the early 1960s, Al Hollingsworth painted angry works such as his *Cry City.* Today a certain gentleness is evident in his paintings, as well as in his thinking and behavior. "I'm not so angry now," he says with a smile.

Hollingsworth has always been an innovator in regard to media. His *Cry City* is a collage made of egg crates, and, he is constantly experimenting. He prepared his doctoral thesis at New York University on the use of adhesives in collage, and he has found exciting new uses for fluorescent paints.

Whatever their message, the younger black artists are keeping up with the evolving language of modern art and have expressed a fascinating kaleidoscope of emotions in a variety of ways—Op, Pop, hard-edge, abstract, collage, and montage have all poured forth from their studios. The sculptors, too, have shown their inventiveness in every media from traditional plaster, clay, wood, and stone to more modern materials that vary from sculptural assemblages of found objects to fantasies in forged steel or aluminum.

A few artists are extensively involved with the materials and processes that have emerged through developments in science and technology. Working in teams with electricians, scientists, or engineers, they are producing art objects that move, light, change colors, and defy description. Some could be called "kinetic sculpture," and Tom Lloyd's creations have been termed "programmed light," but the piece by Daniel La Rue Johnson, which was recently purchased by the Cleveland Art Museum, is impossible to define.

Many black artists are following a popular trend and are seeking renewed meaning in this technological age by handcrafting useful objects out of natural materials. This is a particularly interesting development when we consider that in doing this the Afro-American is following in the footsteps of his ancestors—African as well as American slave craftsmen. It must be remembered, too, that in joining the craft revival in this country, the black artist is a part of a major art movement in America: one thing that distinguishes twentieth-century American art from that of the preceding century is the concept that art is a combination of beauty and utility. Nineteenth-century reaction to the ugliness created by the Industrial Revolution temporarily obliterated this age-old concept and put art on a pedestal. Now the art world has come full circle back to the original idea that art should be functional. While there still remains a certain amount of snobbery in art circles, and a few diehards cling to the old notion of "art for art's sake," this is fast disappearing. Today there is a growing cooperation between artists, engineers, and industry and a greater appreciation for handmade articles. This trend has led many artists of all races to express themselves through crafts. Recent surveys made jointly by the American Crafts Council and the Old Slave Mart Museum in Charleston, South

*Moskee* by Tom Lloyd; 1967. Electronic sculpture. (30 Contemporary Black Artists Exhibit. Collection of Phillip Morris International)

*Champion* by Benny Andrews; 1967. Oil and collage. (30 Contemporary Black Artists Exhibit. Courtesy of the artist)

*Running Hybrid* by Richard Hunt; 1965. Welded stainless steel. (30 Contemporary Black Artists Exhibit. Dorsky Gallery)

*Draped Head* by William E. Artis. (Harmon Collection in the National Archives)

William E. Artis turning a pot on the wheel. (Courtesy of the artist)

Carolina, have revealed that Afro-Americans are producing beautiful hand-made, useful objects in a number of different media, including ceramics, weaving, jewelry, stitchery, mosaics, enameling, metal arts, glassblowing, and stained-glass.

Sargent Johnson adopted ceramics as his medium before World War II. He was followed, during the war, by William Artis, who is now on the faculty of Mankato State College, Minnesota. A born teacher, Artis has brought an inventive and fresh intellectual approach to his career. His own work shows the influence of Ivan Mestrovic, the expatriate Yugoslav sculptor with whom he studied at Syracuse University.

Other notable ceramists include Jim Kane, Carroll Simms, Hubert Collins, Dale Brockman Davis, Ernest Leroy Herbert, Ben James, Doyle Lane, William Maxwell, Amos White, Howard Mallory, Jim Tanner, Bob Stull, James Mosely, and E. D. Taylor. A number of these artists teach, and combine their production of functional pots with sculpture or glassblowing. Few, if any, use the African method of coiling and molding the pieces by hand; instead, they "throw" their pots on the wheel. Most use glazes, and E. D. Taylor has invented a process of transferring a news article to the ceramic object by impressing it directly into the clay body. He calls the unique results "News Pots."

Many black artists have taken up weaving as a career. Among them are Sheryle Butler, Evangeline Montgomery, Wilhelmina Godfrey, Theresa Allen, Horathel Hall, Athene Watson, Eddie Smith, and Allen Fannin. The latter, a creative weaver, carries on a threefold career—teaching, exhibiting, and designing beautiful original pieces of handspun, handwoven linen or woolen fabrics as samples for industrial mills to copy. He develops new weave constructions for commercial use, and he also designs, weaves, and spins for private customers. Self-taught, this craftsman lectures extensively and is spanning the gaps between industrial design, art education, and gallery exhibition. He has exhibited, from coast to coast, collections of original work; all of these are newly created for each occasion. This is just one example of the way in which a handcraftsman can put his talents to use both for fine art as well as for industry.

Jewelry-making also is a popular handcraft. A recent exhibit at Mills College Art Gallery, in Oakland, California, listed five black California craftsmen in this field, one of whom works in wood. In the East are several others, including Constance Ramsey, a member of the Society of Connecticut Craftsmen, and Art Smith, whose work was included in the Johnson Collection, OBJECTS: USA.

Gloria Bohanan of Oakland, California, and Evelyn Mitchell of Cleveland, Ohio, work in stitchery. Ellen Banks Woodsum, of Boston, and Florence Staats, of New Jersey, produce interesting rugs and wall hangings. Ibibio Fundi, of Berkeley, makes wooden reliefs, and both Donald Stinson and Eileen Abdulrashid do enameling.

Dr. Leo Twiggs, of Orangeburg, South Carolina, has adapted the ancient art of batik to the creation of framed pictures. Twigg's technique is almost identical to that used in Africa and the Orient. Working from a sketch, details of the picture are brush-painted with dyes onto unbleached muslin. An application of hot wax prevents them from absorbing more color when the cloth is dipped into dye for background or area color. Some batiks may require twenty or more dippings of various dyes. On occasion, the batik is completely covered with hot wax and placed in a freezer until cold. Then certain parts are crushed to obtain a crackled effect. A completed batik is ironed between newspapers to remove the wax.

Ceramic by Carrol Simms. White with high textures like tree bark made by mixing bristol glaze with earth-brown slips and oxides. (Courtesy of the artist)

Creative pottery by Amos White. (Courtesy of the artist.)

Stoneware cookie jar by Carroll Simms. (Courtesy of the artist)

Ceramic vase by Amos White. (Courtesy of the artist)

Stained-glass window by Douglas Phillips for St. Thomas Rectory, Cleveland, Ohio. Phillips solved his space problem by dividing the area under the peaked roof into panels knit together by swaths suggesting movement. (Photo, courtesy of the artist)

Spinner-weavers Allen and Dotty Fannin beside the loom which Mr. Fannin designed and built. (Photo, courtesy of the artists)

Douglas Phillips of Cleveland, Ohio, operates one of the very few stained-glass studios in the entire country, and he has made windows for churches, public buildings, and private homes. He employs many assistants, both Negro and Caucasian, in following the steps necessary to execute a window. These include designing the window, drawing it to scale, making kraft-paper patterns from which the stained glass is cut, and, finally, glazing, or assembling. Phillips practices his traditional art with a contemporary flair. Though he uses old techniques, he does not try to reproduce medieval windows, because today's architecture calls for different, usually abstract, effects. The freedom of contemporary art allows for brilliant splashes of color held together by sweeping lines that suggest movement. The Phillips Studio also produces both liturgical and secular windows with faceted glass. This method achieves rich, bold effects by setting various shapes of thick, jewel-like chunks of glass into concrete. An added dimension results, because the glass both reflects light and glows from light sources behind it.

There are, in fact, so many different branches of art and craft into which Negroes have ventured that one is no longer surprised to hear of a new instance. Today they are involved in practically every branch of art in America. Afro-Americans have distinguished themselves not only as gallery, or easel artists and as handcraftsmen, but also as interior, dress, and furniture designers; as architects and landscape architects; in commercial and industrial art; and as illustrators. James Allen set the pace for Negro photographers in the creative arts, and photographers such as Gordon Parks and Gordon Parks, Jr. and others have followed.

Although today's Negro artists are becoming more and more sophisticated, fine primitives come to the fore from time to time. The dream-inspired pictures of untutored Minnie Evans, of Wilmington, North Carolina, are fascinating and certainly as valuable and unique a contribution to American art as the work of such earlier primitives as Horace Pippin and William Edmondson. Hugh Moore, formerly a porter at the Cleveland Art Museum, asked permission to take home scraps of modeling clay, and so began his career as a sculptor. His ceramic birds have been sold in museums throughout the country. And the painter Teddy Gunn, a member of the Harlem Cultural Commission, has consistently refused invitations to study, because he believes "art within the human being has got to flow free," and he fears that study will inhibit this freedom.

There are, of course, many commercial craftsmen who have little hope of improving their education or economic condition and who continue to turn out excellent artistic work in masonry, wrought iron, putty modeling, cabinet-making, and the like, just as their ancestors did. Many of them, like Phillip Simmons of Charleston, South Carolina, learned their craft from slaves or ex-slaves. Simmons was apprenticed at the age of thirteen to Peter Simmons—no relation—who had been born a slave. He works on an ancient anvil mounted on a block of wood and his vise is at least 150 years old. But the crudeness of his shop is not reflected in his work, which is mostly ornamental ironwork of great originality and beauty designed by Mr. Simmons himself. One of the most sought-after cabinetmakers in Charleston was the late Walter S. Noisette, born shortly after the Civil War. He did all the carving, fitting, and finishing by hand on furniture of his own design. And one of the most unsung craftsmen of all is the vanishing "handyman," like Peter Alston, of Awendaw, South Carolina, whose versatility, skillful craftsmanship, and creative ingenuity enable him to turn with equal facility from masonry to carpentry to imaginative arrangements of museum exhibits in The Old Slave Mart Museum in Charleston, where he works.

Obtaining publicity and selling work is always a problem for artists, and one of the more significant developments of recent years is the entrance of business and industry into art patronage. As far back as 1943, the Fine Arts Department of International Business Machines purchased some thirty-two paintings, prints, and sculptures by Negro artists. Other concerns that have acted as patrons are Philip Morris International and the American Greeting Card Company. The latter's exhibit in the spring of 1968, called "New Voices," was such a success that the Minneapolis Institute of Arts had it expanded and it opened in the Minneapolis Institute in October 1968, followed by a coast-to-coast tour of seven major art museums across the country, with the title "30 Contemporary Black Artists."

In the past, the reluctance of Negro artists to label themselves by race, plus the difficulty of identifying the maker in his work, have prevented Afro-Americans as a racial group from receiving the credit they deserve in the art world. When an artist does reach the top, the general public often does not know whether he is black or white. The upswing in group shows of black artists lately has helped to rectify this oversight. Several retrospective exhibits have been organized by colleges and universities and these have received wide publicity through reports in art magazines and newspapers. Even the more staid and conservative art galleries across the country are featuring the work of Afro-Americans, both established professionals and untrained neighborhood artists. Such shows have been held recently in the Cleveland Art Museum, the Smithsonian Institute, the Museum of Modern Art, and the Metropolitan Museum of Art. Unfortunately, these Caucasian-dominated museums are finding it hard to catch up on years of ignorance concerning Negro art and artists. Their well-meaning attempts to make up for their long neglect have sometimes had just the opposite effect. The elaborate "Harlem on my Mind" show held at the Metropolitan, which received much adverse criticism, is just one example.

The art establishment is also guilty of some glaring oversights. A recent example occurred in New York, where an important museum held a retrospective of "American Art of the 30s." Not one black artist was represented! Such omissions are hard to understand, much less justify. Perhaps the Negro response to this oversight explains it best of all. Angered over this slight to black artists, a counter-show was organized and held in Harlem's new Studio Museum. Its title, "Invisible Americans: Black Arts of the 30s," referred to Ralph Ellison's book, *The Invisible Man,* a superb discussion of the exclusion of blacks from consciousness by the white establishment. Henri Ghent, Director of the Brooklyn Museum's Community Gallery, commented, "They refuse to see us. Small wonder our artists have not been taken seriously."

The Harlem Studio Museum itself is an important new concept in community museums. Its three-part program includes a filmmaking project; exhibitions of both a scholarly and documentary nature organized by guest directors who are experts in their fields; and, most important, an effort to bring artist and people directly together, enlarging the context of the creative act to include the audience itself. Thanks to an enthusiastic board of directors and an unprecedented response from the community at large, it appears to be succeeding. This is very much a community project in which the whole neighborhood participates. It is *their* museum and they support it in many ways. Yet at the

*Code* by Allen and Dotty Fannin. Hand-spun cyanamid acrylic fiber, unspun rayon staple fiber, monofilament by Gudebrod. (Photo, courtesy of the artists)

Theresa Pratt Allen, artist-weaver at Texas Southern University Art Department, at the loom. (Courtesy of the artist)

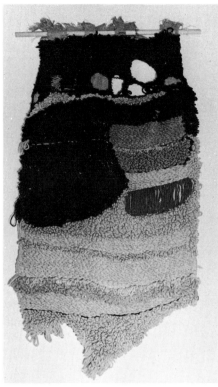

*Black Experience,* wall hanging by Florence Staats. (Photo, courtesy of the artist)

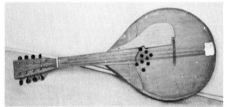

*Spiritualin* by Joseph Armstrong. This instrument was given its name because "the idea was given by the spirit." The back and front were made of old cypress shingles, the sides of maple wood from venetian blinds, the keyboard of top-oak from a stair rail. Material for the keys was the only part bought. (Courtesy, Kiah Museum of Negro Art)

same time the quality of the shows put on so far is earning it the respect of the critics and the art establishment. It has even been said that the two most significant events to affect the entire art world in recent years are the "Thirty Contemporary Black Artists" exhibit and the opening of the Studio Museum in Harlem.

Negro art patronage such as this is encouraging. Initiative for the establishment and support of black artists' groups and exhibits comes with increasing frequency from Afro-Americans themselves. People in Harlem call this a "grass-roots" movement, and it is evident in many communities and throughout many levels of society. Some of these have been in existence for many years, and it is significant that such organizations as the South Side Community Art Center, founded through the help of the Federal Arts Programs, and Karamu House, which began with the efforts of two white social workers, have survived because they have the support of the Negro community.

In Chicago, the street fairs, such as the Lake Meadows Art Fair founded by Marion Perkins, Bernard Goss, and others, have for some time been a major showcase for black artists. The Spiral Group in New York and the Conference of Artists, which is now eleven years old, are two other organizations that were originated by Negroes. Noah Purifoy and Judson Powell have tried, through Studio Watts in Los Angeles, "to demonstrate to the community of Watts, to Los Angeles, and to the world at large, that education through creativity is the only way left for a person to find himself in this materialistic world." Virginia Kiah in Savannah, Georgia, and Margaret Burroughs in Chicago have both opened Museums of Negro Art. And in New York, small galleries and Sunday "salons" in private homes have sprung up, and black community leaders have taken over where the white establishment leaves off.

Naturally, some of this grass-roots movement is linked to the popularity of the African theme among Afro-Americans. Some artists and art galleries have taken African names. Many black artists and craftsmen are adapting African patterns and techniques to their own work; the African art of tie-dye is especially popular among the young and is used for everything from scarves to jeans. Direct importation of African clothes like dashikis and kaftans is now giving place to more imaginative Afro-American articles of dress—a blend of the Old World and the New—created by youthful black designers. African designs taken from wood, basketry, and fabrics are also being adapted to American use. Some of the jewelry currently being made in the Bedford-Stuyvesant section of New York in tiny, crude, African-type forges, on sidewalks or in storefront studios, is fascinating. Utilizing the simplest tools, the craftsmen make their jewelry of aluminum wire, seeds, bone, beads, gold, or silver, with astonishing results.

Lacking a thorough knowledge of their own cultural history, many of these young people are using East African themes as readily as West African ones in the mistaken notion that they are reverting to their ancestral culture. Nonetheless, the results are exciting.

The more recent clamor for black studies programs has led to Afro-American cultural centers in many of the colleges and universities; students can thus see exhibits of African art and display their own work. It has also led to such organizations as the Harlem group that calls itself "African Americans For Friendship and Retaining of our Image, Culture, and Arts," whose purposes are implicit in the name. There seems little doubt, as Professor Jack Jordan has said, that "the quickening of concern for things black has made the time ripe for Negro advancement in art."

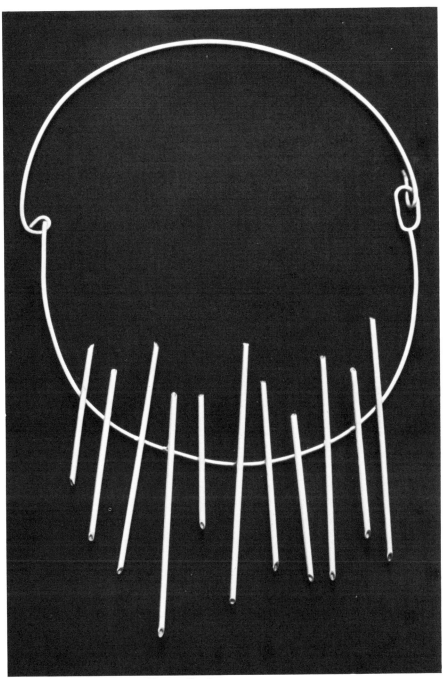

Silver tube necklace by Constance Ramsey. (Courtesy
of the artist)

Jewelry made by black craftsmen in Bedford-Stuyvesant, N.Y. (Collection Old Slave Mart Museum.
Photo, author)

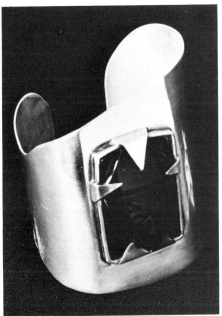

Bracelet, sterling with obsidian stone, by Constance
Ramsey.

*Market Women, Ghana* by John Biggers. Illustration from the artist's book, *Ananse*. (Photo, courtesy of the artist)

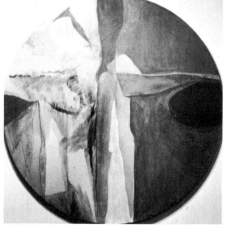

*Reaching For Center* by Betty Blayton, 1969. Oil collage, 58" diameter.

*Icons and Gods* by Raymond Saunders. 1968. Oil collage, 78" x 62½". (Courtesy, Terry Dintenfass Gallery)

It may well be that this racial conciousness is the most significant development of the contemporary art scene, as it was during the Negro Renaissance. It is certainly responsible for the resurgence of black patronage, and for the spirit of self-confidence that is leading many black artists into innovative and unorthodox fields. Willingness to accept racial identification is resulting in greater publicity and respect for the talents of black artists, and this in turn gives encouragement to the rising generation of talented young Negroes. There is no doubt, too, that identification with African craftsmen is at least partly responsible for the growing number of young black men and women who have adopted handcrafts as a means of expressing themselves.

Black youth of America, vitally aware of their potential, can find art a powerful vehicle not only to express their history but also to project their destiny. They are fortunate in having a cultural heritage from two great sources —the Old World of Africa, and the New World of the United States. As Americans, they must never lose sight of one anymore than they should of the other. White America also has a duty. It must not forget that, segregated though he has been, the black man has been an American from the very earliest days of this country. He has contributed to our history, defense, economic progress, science, technology, government, education, and, above all, to the arts. He must no longer be the "Invisible American," and men of all races must see to it that this is so.

We may not have kept pace with one another in the past, but in spite of our regular failures, our regular missteps, we must keep moving forward together.

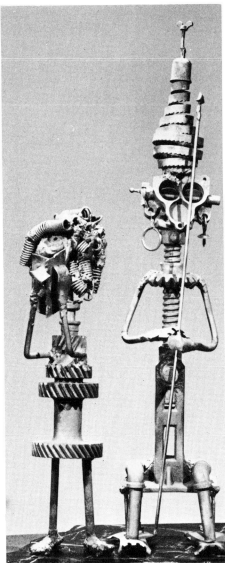

*African Decree* by Jack Jordan. Made of "found" objects. (Courtesy of the artist)

*Preacher* by Charles White, 1952. Ink drawing. (Collection of Whitney Museum of American Art, New York)

# BIBLIOGRAPHY

Up to this time there has been no single, reliable study of Afro-American cultural history. The reader who wishes to know more of subject must seek his information from a variety of sources.

The following is a list of some of the more useful and available English-language sources I have used, but is comprehensive in no other sense. A few titles are obtainable in paperback. Many of the books contain excellent bibliographies to help readers who wish to pursue a subject in greater depth.

The books are grouped under the heading of the chapters to which they mainly apply; but there is necessarily some overlapping of subject matter.

## 1. African Background

There are many sources for this section, but few that are succint, easily read, or trustworthy. The accounts of early travelers, explorers, or missionaries are sometimes fascinating, sometimes dull, frequently biased; the background and audience of the writer must always be kept in view. They are helpful, however, if accepted with caution. Most histories and art histories have in the past confined themselves to Ancient Egypt and regarded Black Africa as without culture or history of note. Fortunately, increased interest in Africa has recently produced a number of new books that are more objective and broader in scope.

Balandier, Georges. *Daily Life in the Kingdom of the Kongo from the 16th to 18th Century.* New York: Pantheon, 1968.
Bohannan, Paul. *Africa and the Africans.* Garden City: Natural History Press, 1964.
Cary, Joyce. *Britain and West Africa.* London: Longmans, Green, 1947.
Coughlan, Robert. *Tropical Africa* Life World Library. New York: Time Inc., 1963.
Darbois, Dominique, and V. Vasut. *African Dance.* Prague: Artia, 1962.
Davidson, Basil. *The Lost Cities of Africa.* Boston: Little, Brown, 1959.
.................................. *Black Mother.* Boston: Little, Brown, 1961.
.................................. *Africa: History of a Continent.* New York: Macmillan, 1966.
................... *F. K. Buah, and J. F. Ajayi. A History of West Africa to the Nineteenth Century.* Garden City: Anchor Books, Doubleday, 1966.
Ibn Batuta [Mohammed ibn Abd Allah]. *Travels in Asia and Africa 1325–1354.* Trans. by H. A. R. Gibb. London: Routledge, 1929.
Labouret, Henri. *Africa Before The White Man.* Trans. by Francis Huxley. New York: Walker, 1962.
Lhote, Henri. "Discovering a Stone Age Museum," *Horizon*, May 1959, p. 72.
Lystad, Robert A. *The Ashanti, A Proud People.* New Brunswick: Rutgers, 1958.
Mellaart, James. "Man's First Murals," *Horizon*, Sept. 1962, p. 11.
Murdock, George Peter. *Africa, Its People and Their Cultural History.* New York: McGraw-Hill, 1959.
Oliver, Roland, and J. D. Fage. *A Short History of Africa.* Baltimore: Penguin, 1966.
Shinnie, P. L. *Meroë.* New York: Praeger, 1967.
Vansina, Jan. *Kingdoms of the Savanna.* Madison: University of Wisconsin, 1966.
Wiedner, Donald L. *A History of Africa South of the Sahara.* New York: Random House, 1962.
Woodson, Carter Godwin. *African Heroes and Heroines.* Washington, D. C.: Associated Publishers, 1944.

## 2. West African Art and Craft

The reader will have no trouble finding books on traditional African art, and since the finest examples come from West Africa, most of them are relevant to Afro-Americans. However, to be certain of the exceptions, some knowledge of the location of tribes and their reference to the slaving area is necessary. For location of tribes, Murdock's *Africa, Its People and Their Cultural History* mentioned in the previous section contains a useful list of all African tribes and subtribes and their areas; for information about the slaving area, see the references in this section. It should also be kept in mind that tribes are sometimes mentioned without the prefix *Ba,* which means "people of." Thus, *Kuba* and *Bakuba* refer to the same tribe. Books on African art sometimes list the same object variously: for instance, under the tribal origin (Mende), the society for which it was made (Bundu), or the country (Sierra Leone). In addition, spelling of tribal names varies. *Bachokwe* has been spelled twenty-eight different ways! With these pitfalls kept in mind, many fine sources are available, including catalogs of exhibitions.

Carroll, Kevin. *Yoruba Religious Carving.* New York: Praeger, 1967.
Cole, Herbert M., and Robert Farris Thompson. *Bibliography of Yoruba Sculpture.* New York: Museum of Primitive Art, New York Graphic, 1964.
Eliade, Mircea. *The Forge and the Crucible.* Trans. by Stephen Corrin. New York: Harper, 1962.
Gardi, René. *African Crafts and Craftsmen.* Trans. by Sigrid MacRae. New York: Van Nostrand Reinhold, 1969.
Hambly, Wilfrid D. *Clever Hands of the African Negro.* Washington, D. C.: Associated Publishers, 1945.
Harley, George W. "Masks as Agents of Social Control in Northeast Liberia." In *Papers of the Peabody Museum of American Archaeology and Ethnology* vol. 32, no. 2. Cambridge, Mass: Harvard University, 1950.
Leuzinger, Elsy. *The Art of Africa.* New York: Greystone, 1967.
Rachewiltz, Boris de. *Introduction to African Art.* New York: New American Library, 1966.
Robbins, Warren. *African Art in American Collections.* New York: Praeger, 1966.
Schwab, George. "Tribes of the Liberian Hinterland." Edited by George W. Harley. In *Papers of the Peabody Museum of American Archaeology and Ethnology* vol. 31. Cambridge, Mass: Harvard University, 1947.
Segy, Ladislas. *African Sculpture.* New York: Dover, 1958.
.................... *African Sculpture Speaks.* New York: Lawrence Hill, 1955.
Trowell, Margaret. *African Design.* New York: Prager, 1960.
.......................... , and Hans Nevermann. *African and Oceanic Art.* Rev. ed. New York: Abrams, 1965.

### CATALOGS

*African Negro Art.* Herring, James V. Howard University Gallery of Art, Founders Library, Washington, D. C., 1953.
*African Tribal Images.* Fagg, William. The Katherine White Reswick Collection, Cleveland Museum of Art, 1968.
*African Tribal Sculpture.* Plass, Margaret. The University Museum, Philadelphia, 1956.
*Impact Africa—African Art and the West.* The Inaugural Exhibition of the Bernice McIlhenny Wintersteen Student Center, Philadelphia Museum of Art, 1969.
*Sculpture from Africa.* The Museum of Primitive Art, New York, 1968.
*Sculpture of Black Africa.* Siever, Roy and Arnold Rubin. The Paul Tishman Collection, Los Angeles County Museum of Art, 1969.

*Senufo Sculpture from West Africa.* The Museum of Primitive Art, New York, 1963.
*The Clark and Frances Stillman Collection of Congolese Sculpture.* The Museum of Primitive Art, New York, 1966.
*The Language of African Art.* A Guest Exhibition of the Museum of African Art at the Smithsonian Institution, Fine Arts and Portrait Gallery Building, 1970.
*Traditional African Art.* The Peabody Museum, Harvard University and Museum of African Art, Washington, D.C., 1966.

## 3. Transition

Many books have been written about the African derivations of American Negro music, dance, and folklore; and Dr. Lorenzo Turner's study of linguistics is well known. However, little study has been made of Africanisms in the field of the plastic arts, so it is difficult to find helpful books on the subject. Herskovits's classic *Myth of the Negro Past* is still the best general reference book, covering religion, social structure, folklore, language, and handcrafts, among other subjects.

Carawan. Guy and Candie. *Ain't You Got a Right to the Tree of Life?* New York: Simon and Schuster, 1966.
DuBois, W. E. B. *The Souls of Black Folk, Essays and Sketches,* Chicago: McClurg, 1903.
.................................. . *The Gift of Black Folk.* Boston: Stratford, 1924.
Fisher, Miles Mark. *Negro Slave Songs in the U.S.* New York: Citadel, 1963.
Gonzales, Ambrose E. *The Black Border—Gullah Stories of The Carolina Coast.* Columbia: State, 1922.
Hare, Maud Cuney. *Negro Musicians and Their Music.* Washington, D.C.: Associated Publishers, 1936.
Herskovits, Melville J. *The Myth of the Negro Past.* Boston: Beacon, 1958.
Hughes, Langston, and Arna Bontemps, eds. *The Book of Negro Folklore.* New York: Dodd, Mead, 1965.
Jones, Leroi. *The Blues People.* New York: Morrow, 1963.
Work, John W., ed. *American Negro Songs and Spirituals.* New York: Bonanza, 1940.

## 4, 5. Slave Craftsmen

Much of the material for these chapters was obtained through original sources. Field work included interviews with the descendants of slaves and of slaveholders, visits to plantations and contemporary Negro craftsmen. The collection of the late Miriam B. Wilson, founder of The Old Slave Mart Museum, was invaluable: it contains not only slave-made handcrafts whose provenance is clear, but original documents, photostats, maps, letters, engravings, newspaper clippings, and card reference files, as well as personal notes and information based on Miss Wilson's thirty years' interest in this subject.

### General Background

Bancroft, Frederic. *Slave Trading in the Old South.* New York: Ungar, 1931.
Doar, David. "Rice and Rice Planting in The South Carolina Low Country." *Contributions from the Charleston Museum,* ed. by E. Milby Burton. Charleston, S.C.: The Charleston Museum, 1936.
Easterby, J. H. *The South Carolina Rice Plantations.* Chicago: University of Chicago, 1945.
Franklin, John Hope. *From Slavery to Freedom.* New York: Knopf, 1964.
Heyward, Duncan Clinch. *Seed from Madagascar.* Chapel Hill: University of North Carolina, 1937.

Hugues, Langston, and Milton Meltzer. *A Pictorial History of the Negro in America.* New York: Crown, 1956.

Lofton, John. *Insurrection in South Carolina, The Turbulent World of Denmark Vesey.* Yellow Springs: Antioch Press, 1964.

Mannix, Daniel P., and Malcolm Cowley. *Black Cargoes—A History of the Atlantic Slave Trade, 1518-1865.* New York: Viking, 1962.

Olmsted, Frederick Law. *The Slave States.* New York: Capricorn, 1959.

Perkerson, Medora Field. *White Columns in Georgia.* New York: Reinhart, 1952.

Phillips, Ulrich Bonnell. *American Negro Slavery.* New York: Appleton-Century, 1940.

................................... . *Life and Labor in the Old South.* Boston: Little, Brown, 1941.

Purse, R. S., ed. *Charleston City Directory and Stranger's Guide, for 1856.* New York: J. F. Trow, Printer.

Quarles, Benjamin. *The Negro in the Making of America.* New York: Collier, 1966.

Ravenel, Beatrice St. Julien. *Architects of Charleston.* Charleston: Carolina Art Association, 1945.

Stampp, Kenneth M. *The Peculiar Institution.* New York: Knopf, 1963.

Stoney, Samuel Gaillard. *Plantations of the Low Country.* Charleston: Carolina Art Association, 1938.

Wade, Richard Clement. *Slavery in the Cities: The South, 1820-1860.* New York: Oxford University, 1964.

Walsh, Richard. *Charleston's Sons of Liberty.* Columbia: University of South Carolina, 1959.

Crafts and Craftsmanship

Bowles, Ella Shannon. *Homespun Handicrafts* Philadelphia: Lippincott, 1931.

Deas, Alston and Richard J. Bryan. *The Early Ironwork of Charleston.* Columbia: Bostick & Thornley, 1941.

Earle, Alice Morse. *Home Life in Colonial Days.* New York: Macmillan, 1898.

Hall, Eliza Calvert [Obenchain]. *A Book of Hand-Woven Coverlets.* Boston: Little, Brown, 1931.

Harllee, W. C. *Kinfolks.* Vol. I. Caroliniana Library. Columbia: University of South Carolina, 1934.

Jones, Louis C., and Marshall B. Davidson. "American Folk Art In Fenimore House, Cooperstown, N.Y." Album LZ, The Metropolitan Museum of Art Miniatures.

Peto, Florence. *American Coverlets and Quilts.* New York: Chanticleer, 1949.

Prime, Alfred Coxe. *The Arts and Crafts in Philadelphia Maryland and South Carolina 1721—1785,* and *1786—1800.* Series One and Two. New York, Plenum, DaCapo, 1926 and 1932.

Regensteiner, Else. *The Art of Weaving.* New York: Van Nostrand Reinhold, 1970.

Tunis, Edwin. *Colonial Craftsmen and the Beginnings of American Industry.* Cleveland: World, 1965.

Webster, Marie D. *Quilts, Their Story and How to Make Them.* Marion, Indiana: Marie D. Webster, 1929.

## 6, 7, 8. Afro-American Art and Craft

I have found no standard art history that refers to a single Afro-American artist! References to African art were lacking, or scanty and patronizing. (In the widely used *Art Through the Ages* by Helen Gardner, the Benin bronzes are attributed to Portuguese influence!) Two books on Afro-American artists should be noted: Porter's *Modern Negro Art* and Dover's *American Negro Art.* Both are extremely useful. The Old Slave Mart Museum Collection of catalogs and pamphlets provided by the Harmon Foundation have proved invaluable, as have the catalogs of some of the more recent exhibits of the work of Afro-American artists.

Blodgett, Geoffery. "John Mercer Langston and the Case of Edmonia Lewis: Oberlin—1862." *The Journal of Negro History,* vol. 53, (1968) no. 3.

Butcher, Margaret Just. *The Negro in American Culture.* New York: Knopf, 1956.

Dover, Cedric. *American Negro Art.* Greenwich: New York Graphic Society, 1960.

Greene, Carroll, Jr. "The Afro-American Artist." *The Art Gallery Magazine,* April, 1968, p. 12.

Hughes, Langston. "The Twenties: Harlem and Its Negritude," *African Forum,* vol. 1, no. 4 p. 11.

Kamarck, Edward, Ed. *Arts in Society: The Arts and the Black Revolution.* Research Studies and Development in the Arts. Madison: University of Wisconsin, 1968.

Landy, Jacob, "William H. Johnson: Expressionist Turned 'Primitive'," *Journal of the American Association of University Women,* vol. 51 (1958), no. 3.

Locke, Alain. "Up Till Now," *The Negro Artist Comes of Age.* A National Survey of Contemporary American Artist. Albany Institute of History and Art.

Moore, Trevor Wyatt. "Not in Black and White," *Ave Maria,* July 22, 1967, p. 8.

Pleasants, J. Hall. "Joshua Johnston, the First American Negro Portrait Painter." *The Maryland Historical Magazine,* vol. 37, (1942), no. 2, p. 121.

Porter, James A. *Modern Negro Art.* New York: Dryden, 1943.

Rose, Alvin W. "Negro Art and the Great Transformation," *Arts in Society,* Fall, 1959, p. 55.

Senghor, Leopold Sedar. "The Function and Meaning of the First World Festival of Negro Arts," *African Forum,* vol. 1, no. 4, p. 5.

CATALOGS

*Charles White, Exhibition of Drawings,* The Gallery of Art, Howard University, 1967.

*Contemporary Art Collection.* Atlanta: Atlanta University, 1942-1959.

*Contemporary Negro Art.* Baltimore: Baltimore Museum of Art, 1939.

*Edward Mitchell Bannister, 1928-1901,* Robbins, Daniel, An Exhibition Organized by the Museum of Art, Rhode Island School of Design for the Museum of African Art, Frederick Douglass Institute, Washington, D.C., 1966.

*Exhibit of Fine Arts: Productions of American Negro Artists.* Harmon Foundation and the Commission on the Church and Race Relations, Federal Council of Churches, International House, New York, 1928.

*Exhibits of Fine Arts by American Negro Artists,* Harmon Foundation and the Commission on the Church and Race Relations, Federal Council of Churches, International House, New York, 1929 and 1930.

*Exhibition of the Work of Negro Artists,* Harmon Foundation at the Art Center, New York, 1931.

*Exhibition of Productions by Negro Artists,* Harmon Foundation at the Art Center, New York, 1933.

*Negro Artists, An Illustrated Review of Their Achievements.* Harmon Foundation, New York, 1935.

*10 Afro-American Artists of the 19th Century,* Porter, James, Howard University, Washington, D.C., 1967.

*10 Negro Artists From the U.S.* The United States Committee for the First World Festival of Negro Arts, Inc., and the National Collection of Fine Arts, Smithsonian Institution. Dakar, Senegal, 1966.

*The Evolution of Afro-American Artists—1800-1950,* City University of New York in cooperation with Harlem Cultural Council and New York Urban League, 1967.

*30 Contemporary Black Artists,* An Exhibition Organized by The Minneapolis Institute of Arts with the Assistance of Ruder & Finn, Inc., New York, The Minneapolis Institute of Arts, 1968.

# INDEX

141